Lakeland to Congo

Lakeland to Congo

The Revival Continues

by

Andrew Snyder and Itumba (Edo) Mukeza

Lakeland to Congo: The Revival Continues
Copyright © 2010
by
Andrew Snyder and Itumba (Edo) Mukeza
ALL RIGHTS RESERVED

Scripture quotations marked (AMP) are taken from the *Amplified Bible*, Copyright © 1954, 1958, 1962, 1964, 1965, 1987 by The Lockman Foundation. Used by permission.

Scripture quotations marked (NIV) are taken from the Holy Bible, New International Version®, NIV®. Copyright © 1973, 1978, 1984 by Biblica, Inc.™ Used by permission of Zondervan. All rights reserved worldwide. www.zondervan.com

Scripture quotations marked (KJV) are taken from the Authorized King James Version of the Bible

First Printing 2010

ISBN 978-0-9827963-0-6
Printed in the United States of America
for worldwide distribution

Contents

Dedication I
Introduction 1

Edo's Testimony 5
The Beginning 35
The Revival 41
On to the Congo - The Chronicles 51
Emails 129

Conclusion 155

Dedication

First and foremost, this book is dedicated to the Lord Jesus. Without his passion on the cross, obviously none of this would be possible.

There are many people in my life that deserve a mention:

My mother, Patricia Snyder who encouraged me through this project, and also helped edit and proofread.

Apostle Al Davis and his wife Prophetess Dorothy Davis for their spiritual guidance in my life.

Pastor Stephen Strader at Ignited Church, Lakeland Florida for his tireless work during the Revival.

All of my friends in the Lord worldwide, especially those at Consuming Fire International Ministry, Sarasota, Florida.

Edo's children, who spent a summer without their mother for the sake of the gospel.

INTRODUCTION

THE first part of this book is about Itumba (Edo) Mukeza, an amazing woman that I met from the Democratic Republic of the Congo. She was born and grew up in Congo, and she now lives in London. She gives some very personal details about the extreme difficulties she faced in her life growing up in the Congo, and how she came to be an evangelist. Her testimony is very relevant and moving. The second half of the book covers the events in our lives from our meeting at a revival in Lakeland, Florida, through the conclusion of the revivals we did together in Congo in August 2008. This book also covers my personal journey in the Lord, from a place of total unbelief to the miraculous. God's goodness is amazing to me still. I am humbled and honored that the Lord could use me to touch and change others forever. It amazes me that He could take me from such a dark place into His marvelous light.

I wasn't exactly the perfect candidate for the job according to the usual way of thinking. I didn't start out with any understanding or faith in the Lord. I didn't know more that one or two Bible verses. I even made an effort to keep from learning the Bible as well. I didn't ever go to seminary or to a big Bible college. I didn't get taught by the best. I didn't learn from the top TV preachers. I wasn't born into a family that even really believed in God. I didn't have any of the qualities that one would consider valuable or necessary when it came to the work of the Lord. No family heritage to speak of, no great education in the subject, no connections, no great speaking skills, no one was there pushing or encouraging me every day. From the normal way of thinking, there weren't many clues that things were going to happen the way they did. I was even surprised myself.

We never read the Bible as a family. Sure, we occasionally went to church when I was very little, but when there were three little children to get ready, it became too difficult for my parents, so they quit. I didn't grasp enough of it to make an impact. I barely remember anything except that I couldn't sit still that long. In my opinion, my parents were not going to church because they were in love with the Lord, it was for the show, and for the connections. I may be wrong, and this may be considered unkind. That is how it appears to me. The whole walk is about sacrifice and pressing in against all difficulties for the sake of the Lord. When it is too difficult to get up on Sunday morning, how committed are you anyway? Thank God Jesus was more committed than we are. Amen.

It is important to say that this is my first book. I don't really like to write, and besides, I was never good at it. I never liked English classes, and I always received poor marks as well. I couldn't diagram a sentence for love or money. I got a C- in business communication in college. You may say that it shows. That is OK with me as well. I didn't want to write books anyway. If you don't like this one, I don't mind. If no one reads this book, and even if no one likes it or even buys it, I can always still say that I wrote a book. That is more than a lot of people can say. I didn't write it because I am such a great writer, or because I always wanted to write a book. I am writing it because to me, the story is so amazing, unusual and compelling that it absolutely had to be told. I believe so strongly that this book had to get out to the public, that it would be wrong for me to withhold this story. Your opinion however, may vary.

I had never set my sights on being a miracle worker. How could I, since I didn't believe in miracles? I started out like most people. Even when I got serious later in life and started going to church, I wanted to see miracles, but the church leaders convinced me that they didn't happen today. I thought all of the TV preachers were full of hogwash for the majority of my life. I am telling you that I absolutely didn't believe in miracles before I was saved, and I didn't even believe in them after I was saved either. I thought it was a deception of the enemy. I even knew the

Bible verses to quote to back up my position as taught by the legalistic religion that I found myself in. God has a way of dealing with stubbornness. Sometimes we call it eating crow.

A friend of mine once told me "If you believe, you will receive, but if you doubt, you will go without." I am sure he heard it someplace else, but it rings so true, that I felt I had to repeat it here in case anyone needs to hear it. Feel free to refer back to the above quote any time you would like. You may find it helpful. As a matter of fact, many of the things that are covered in this book are quite unbelievable on the surface. Be assured that I have relayed the important aspects of this story in the most honest and genuine means possible. Even when the details are sketchy, this is for two reasons. The first reason was the language barrier. There were a lot of things going on around me that I didn't have the details on because I simply didn't understand what was being spoken. Secondly, I didn't realize at the time I was writing an account of my trip that I was going to turn this into a book. A lack of details, and in some cases names and addresses doesn't detract from the story or mean that these things didn't occur as I have said.

Enjoy the book.

Edo's Testimony

{*The following story is taken from the testimony that Evangelist Edo Mukeza gave about her life. The testimony was given in Benin City, Nigeria in Feb of 2010. It is essentially a word for word transcript with very minor corrections here and there. Therefore, the flow of the story has a more conversational feel to it. It is important to note that Edo is no longer married to the man mentioned in this story. She is presently married to a man named Placide, who lives in London.*}

Edo Begins

I want to talk to you about how God took me from where I was to where I am now. We had a revival called "Restoration in the Land ". When God wants to restore a land, He starts with an individual. When God wants to restore a family, He starts with one person. Everything God is starting, He is always starting small. I know that God is restoring your families. God is restoring your country. I want to give you part of my testimony about how God restored me, how He is in the process of restoring my whole family and how He has restored my children and my spiritual children as well.

I want to read in the Bible Matthew 13 verses 24-30.

Edo Said,

"24 Another parable He set forth before them saying the kingdom of God or the Kingdom of heaven is like a man who sowed good seed in his field. 25 But while people were sleeping, his enemy came also and sowed wild wheat, and went on his way. 26 So when the plants sprouted and formed grain, the wild wheat appeared also. 27 And the servant of the owner came to him and said, Sir did you not sow good seed *in your field? Then how does it have wild wheat shoots in it? 28 He replied to them, an enemy has done this. The servant said to him, Then do you want us to go and weed them out? 29 But he said, No, lest in gathering the wild wheat you root up the true wheat along with it. 30 Let them grow together until the harvest; and at the harvest time I will say to the reapers, gather the darnel or the wild wheat first and bind it in bundles to be burned, but gather the wheat into my granary."*

[Note: Edo read the above from the Amplified Bible. She modified it slightly to enhance the understanding of the audience. The Lockman Foundation requires an exact quote which is included below for clarity.]

24Another parable He set forth before them, saying, The kingdom of heaven is like a man who sowed good seed in his field. 25But while he was sleeping, his enemy came and sowed also darnel (weeds resembling wheat) among the wheat, and went on his way. 26So when the plants sprouted and formed grain, the darnel (weeds) appeared also. 27And the servants of the owner came to him and said, Sir, did you not sow good seed in your field? Then how does it have darnel shoots in it? 28He replied to them, An enemy has done this. The servants said to him, Then do you want us to go and weed them out? 29But he said, No, lest in gathering the wild wheat (weeds resembling wheat), you root up the [true] wheat along with it. 30Let them grow together until the harvest; and at harvest time I will say to the reapers, Gather the darnel first and bind it in bundles to be burned, but gather the wheat into my granary. Amp.

When Jesus was talking to the disciples as well as to other people he used to speak to them in parables. Parables are stories that relate something that is in the natural world to something spiritual that he is talking about. In this parable, he is talking about the kingdom of God; he is telling them what the kingdom of God looks like as he tells these parables. When you carry on reading you can see that he gives the explanation of this parable. He says that the field that they sow seed into is the world, and God is the sower of good seed. Satan is the sower of bad seed. Now, when Satan comes into the world, he is not going to sow seed into the literal ground, he is going to sow seed into people. This is because peoples lives are what he seeks to destroy. The purpose that God has set us to, that is good seed.

When God created you, when God created me, he created us with a purpose. He created me knowing already before I was even born what I am going to be and what I am going to do. You might ask "what is my purpose on this earth?" God doesn't create somebody and then after start looking and say hmm, you are big, you are tall what shall I make you? No, he has everything already in place, and that is what your life looks like. When you are born, you have already everything planned, now all you have to do is put yourself in the path of God and start following that purpose. We all know that God doesn't create anything useless, so you are not useless, I am not useless. There is no mistake with God. A child is born, maybe out of wedlock. You were not married, you got pregnant and you call that child an accident. With God there is no accident. That child was supposed to be born and has a purpose.

Today the biggest preacher in Uganda is an abandoned child. He was found in a dump. No mother, no father. Today he is the one leading Uganda, he is the biggest preacher, winning people to Christ gathering even the President, even the president's wife into the church to pray. An abandoned child, he was not an accident. Maybe someone told you that you are an accident, maybe someone told you that you are useless maybe someone told you that you are good for nothing. See, those words are the seed of the enemy. Those words are the biggest seed and sometimes we take it lightly. We say things to our children, we say "What are you going to do, what can you give me, by the time you start making your money I'm already dead. You are not going to give me anything, when you are getting married you are going to take care of your son, or of your wife or of your husband you are not going to look after me." We say those words lightly, but we don't know that we are binding the future.

I have seen people that have turned homosexual because someone looked at them, they are a boy and someone looked at them and said "You look like a girl." They said it lightly, but the seed is planted. You see, Satan is not going to present himself and say "I am going to plant an evil seed in you" he takes word, he takes action, he takes things, small, small things that are coming from our mouths, puts it into people and that seed starts to grow, and he turns you into something that you were not supposed to be. Something that God didn't create you to be. He put that seed in you and you turn yourself around and instead of following God, you start following what people are telling you. You start to listen to what people are telling you. In my life it is exactly the same way that the enemy did it to me.

I was born in Congo in a small, small village where there is no running water, and no electricity. Here you have wells, you even have electricity to draw water. In my village we used to go fetch water from the river. We cooked on wood and on charcoal, there was no such thing as a cooker, no such thing as electricity, it wasn't there. Until now it is still the same. There is a little bit of running water from the tap, it runs about two hours every day. You have to take it and store it in the house until you need it the next day. It is also possible that maybe you will go a week without any water.

It was a very, very far away village where I was a little girl walking with no shoes playing around in the dust just like any village child that you can see, that is me. My mom was a Catholic, and just like every good Catholic she would go to church, she would take us to church but when she comes back home, she leaves God in the church. She used to leave God in the church and would go home empty handed. Most of us do that, we come to church we sing, we praise but afterwards we just go out the door, and God stays there. We go empty handed and after we are gone we start talking and living like people that don't know God.

My mom used to look at me and say "You are ugly, I have never seen any ugly child like you." Do you understand? For a young girl to hear somebody telling you that you are ugly that takes your self esteem lower than zero. You don't want to look at anybody, you become timid, you become shy because you know that if I look at somebody that they will say that you are ugly. As a result you don't want to look at anybody. Bad people like to take advantage of kids in that situation because they know that these children don't have the courage to confront them or say no to their face. These bad people will do anything they want to do to you because they know that you are not going to open your mouth. So those words were coming in me everyday. Every time I would be silly, every time I would do something wrong my mother would use that opportunity to put me down and to say things unkind.

I look like my brother, and I look like my mom. My moms dead now, but my father is still alive and I have a big family. I am not saying that my family is bad, what I am saying is that without God a human being is capable of anything. Without God people can do silly things that you have no idea about. We need God in our families, we need the true God. We don't need the *(far away)* God that everyone worships, I need my God, I need my savior. Not the Savior of my pastor, not the Savior of my church, but my personal savior that I can have a relationship with, it doesn't matter where I am or where I have been.

So, all those things that were coming to me, all these things that were just bringing my self esteem down, I just became a very shy person. I didn't look at people in their faces, I didn't speak, I was close to myself, I didn't smile. Part of the reason that I didn't smile was because my mom used to tell me..... we have, I don't know if you have it here. We have vases made of clay and we cook in them. Those vases have an opening like a flower pot, and my mother used to look at me and say that "your lips look like those vases" I would look at those vases and I would say my God, my lips look like that, I better not open them. Because she said that I would walk around with my mouth shut. I didn't want to open my lips, and I didn't want to smile because I knew that if I smiled then somebody was going to look at my ugly lips and they were going to say something.

Now the things that happened to me, I am not telling you a sad story I am going to show you the power of God, I want to show you what God is able to do.

When I was 9 years old....Mothers listen to me, when I was 9 years old my mother used to send the housekeeper to put me to bed. You see, when people are talking outside and it is nearly bedtime in my village they would sit down and they would tell stories and you would laugh and you would cry and you would do all sorts of things. The youngest would fall asleep during the story telling time and my mother would tell the housekeeper to pick me up and take me to bed.

You don't know who you give control of your child to. When you hand your child to somebody, you have given them power over your child. The only thing you can do.... always, especially Christians I ask you to always to pray over your children protect your children with prayers and the blood of Christ because you don't know what the enemy wants to do. You don't know who is going to touch your child. My mother, unfortunately didn't know God, she was just a Christian by name. She handed me to the housekeeper, and the housekeeper put me to bed. When the housekeeper put me to bed, he would molest me sexually. This used to happen to me while I was sleeping. Sometimes when you are sleeping you are half awake and half asleep. You can feel everything, then you are wondering... is this a dream, is this happening to me? Sometimes you don't want to wake up because you don't want it to be true and you have no one to talk to.

Mothers, have some conversation with your children. The only time you talk to your child is when your child is being naughty. You say sternly to your child "You silly boy or girl, you," that is the only time you say anything yet it is not constructive. You don't have time to pick that girl up and hug her and tell her how beautiful she is. Who is going to tell her if you don't tell her? Who is going to comfort that little girl or that little boy that needs love from you? It is you and no one else. You need sometimes to take the time to look them in the eyes and tell them they are beautiful.

I have a beautiful girl, her name is Olivia, she is now 17. She is the most beautiful thing that you have ever seen. If you see me and you see her dad, you would think that she is mixed race. She has green eyes, she is light skinned, tall, thin, she is beautiful, just beautiful. She is my daughter and from when she is born until now I will tell her everyday that "You are beautiful". I am not telling her so that she will become big headed, and believe me, she will not. We parents are sometimes scared that if we tell her like that she will become big headed, but I am telling you no, you are building her self confidence. So I tell her all the time that "you are beautiful". You know that if you don't tell your daughter like that, the first boy that will come and tell her that she is beautiful she is going to run away with him. Do you understand? So it is better if you tell her. So my daughter, and all of my children, I tell them. That way when someone goes and tells my children you are beautiful she is going to say "Thank you, I know, my mom tells me." She is not going to follow a boy around and run away with him because she was told she was beautiful, she knows because I told her.

For me, because I knew I was ugly and I knew I wasn't beautiful so therefore I was worthless and if someone is molesting me so be it, at least somebody takes interest. (*Note: Edo Mukeza is a beautiful woman.*) They must have found something attractive in me. I was 9 years old, I was old enough to open my mouth and tell my mom what was happening, but I did not. The reason is because we did not have dialog, I didn't speak to my mom, and my mom didn't speak to me. I was afraid because I am already a naughty girl. Every time my mom speaks to me she is telling me how naughty I am, how ugly I am. I was afraid that if I went to tell her this person is doing this to me the first thing that I knew my mom would say is "You are a liar". The second thing she would say is that it was because you are naughty, you asked for it. Every day my mom would tell me negative things. For example, you know little girls when you start to notice something in your body you start to notice that you are getting a little bigger and you start to look at yourself, if my mom catches me looking at myself, she would say look at you, prostitute. That was the word she was planting, and later what did I become? A prostitute.

The power of life and death, it is on your tongue. My mom used to criticize me everyday about little things that girls will do. Maybe I would stand and dance, then she would look and instead of being happy that her daughter is enjoying herself she would say " look at this one she is going to be a prostitute, what are you doing that for?" Instead of clapping for the girl, well done, you know how to dance, she used to put me down all the time. So, people took advantage of me. People abused me and I didn't tell my mom anything.

Something happened to me one day. The same housekeeper that molested me stole something from my dad and my dad put him in prison. In my country when you have somebody arrested, you are the one that has to look after them. So, if for example, I accuse you of stealing from me and I take you to the police, while you are in prison, I have to look after you by giving you food and everything. They sent me to go and give the housekeeper food. I am walking in the cell, and there are two men in the cell, the housekeeper and this huge man about 6 feet tall 275 pounds. He had red eyes from smoking marijuana and dancing to the music on the radio in the cell. As a little girl ten years old, I saw him and I trembled. Something shook on the inside of me. I knew this man was a bad man, he scared me to death. I said to myself that I don't want to meet a man like this in my life. I didn't even say that I came to give food to the housekeeper. I dropped the food and ran and ran. Why? Because I was scared of that man. Now, hold onto that thought.

While I was growing, my dad became very angry with me because of my behavior. My behavior was due to the seed of abuse. Do you know what the seed of the sexual abuse does to you? It doesn't make you run away from men, it draws you to men. You become an easy target, anybody that sees you, they want to abuse you sexually and you don't have the power anymore to say no to men. That is what I became. I was running around with boys, and my mom and my dad could not handle it anymore. They were so angry, so upset with me. In my country on your id card they will write the names of your children to tell who they are and who you are. My dad took his ID card, and erased my name and said you are not my child anymore because I was too much to handle. He said "I wash my hands of you, you can go wherever you like, you can do whatever you like, you are not my child anymore." He said something else to me also. He said "If you are my blood if I am your father, you will never amount to anything. If I am not your dad, go ahead, succeed, but I am your dad, you will never succeed." That is a curse and from there I was cursed. Do you know what, my dad can erase my name, but thank God my name is written in the book of life. Jesus came to shed his blood for me. Thank God He redeemed me.

One day, my sister who was married said that she wanted me to go and live with her. My dad had abandoned me, but thank God my sister was still thinking of me. She wanted me to go and live with her. I moved from the village to a big city. I went to live with my sister in the city and within two weeks of my arrival, two people that lived in my sisters house started abusing me sexually in the house. It was as if it was written on my head " Hey, here I am, a target." Two people started abusing me from the house, and when my sister found out, it was my fault. She didn't say "my sister is being abused" She said "You asked for it". By that time I was about 13 years old. My sister said that "My mom told me, my mom warned me, my mom told me already that you are like this. My mom told me that you are a bad girl. Not in my house" and she started cursing me.

When I went to live with her, it was the first time she had seen me in awhile. She thought I was too big of a girl to be in the house because she wanted a little girl to play with her daughter. She didn't want a bigger person. That also was a rejection to me, she rejected me already at the beginning. I was there thinking I am cursed. Everywhere I go it is the same story, I will never go anywhere, I will never amount to anything. Now I am meditating on the curse. I didn't know God, I didn't know anything. That also created rebellion in my heart. I became very stubborn and very rude. If you are looking at me before you said anything, I am already answering you back because I know what you are going to say. It was like I was reading minds. I didn't want anyone to hurt me, so I would hurt them before they could hurt me. I was rude, and my life went on and on and on like that. Trouble followed me everywhere I went. I lived in my uncle's house because my sister couldn't handle me anymore so she sent me to my uncle's house. The day that I arrived, my two cousins from the same dad abused me sexually. I was damaged. Maybe when you see me I am standing, I am preaching, you don't know where I am coming from. You don't know how God has brought me to this point. I was broken. There was no one more broken than I was. I was damaged. I was just walking around the street hoping to die, I just want to die, but death wouldn't come.

One day I had enough. I took pills, a whole bottle of pills. So much that it would kill even a horse. I didn't die. I will tell you what, if God has a purpose for you, the devil cannot take you out. The devil cannot kill you if God has a purpose for you. The second time I took some pills, I didn't die, the third time, the same thing. In different days in different months or years, I didn't die, I couldn't die; the enemy was trying. He knew that God had a purpose for me. He knew that I had a job to do. He knew I would damage his kingdom and I love to do it. The devil knew I was trouble for his kingdom so he was trying to kill me. But people around me didn't understand. I myself didn't understand. That is why I ask the church every time to pray, pray for people that you see on the streets like prostitutes. Put your knees on the floor, beg God to save them. I don't know who was praying for me, I don't know. It wasn't by chance that I am here, someone prayed me through. When you see someone in the church misbehaving, when you see your child going wild don't put them down with bad words, confess good things and bless them pray for them and cover them with prayer.

When I was about 17, 16 turning 17 I became pregnant. By this time my sister sent me back home to my dad because she couldn't handle me, my uncle and his wife couldn't handle me so they sent me back to my dad. My dad looked another way. He said "you are free to stay in my house but I don't know you, I don't know you. Therefore, I was free to go anywhere. I was free to spend nights anywhere that I wanted. Meanwhile, my brother said "I am going to keep paying for you to go to school." I was going to school until my brother said "I don't have money anymore you can't go to school." I don't know about how you do it here. My studies only went until I finished secondary school. I went on to do sewing for one year, and that is it. My whole family, all went to universities and finished except me. I've got four sisters and three brothers, they all have degrees. You know that God sometimes chooses the black sheep of the family. You feel like a black sheep, that is what God likes. When you feel like nothing, God likes to meet you there, take the nothing and show the wisdom, His wisdom instead of the wisdom of the world.

When I was 16 turning 17, I became pregnant with this boyfriend that I had. The boyfriend came home only from boarding school and got me pregnant. Now I am pregnant and he is going back to school. I have no one. Four months pregnant and my dad already said I don't know you. Now I'm wandering the street 4 months pregnant. I have only a little girl's skirt. You know that when you are pregnant you need something to cover with, I have nothing to put on, not even a wrapper. *(A traditional African article of clothing that is essentially a piece of cloth a woman wraps herself in)* I am in a skirt, a little girls skirt and pregnant and nothing to help deal with it.

Now, there was a man in the area; a very powerful man. Everybody seems to be scared of him. Whatever he says goes. He had a big house and he had a lot of people coming over to his house. Whenever he is passing by in the street the people would always move out of his way. Well respected, the people bow when he is passing. I didn't know what the fuss was all about. He came to me one day and said "I like you, I have been liking you for a long time but you didn't pay attention to me because you were too rude because you thought that you came from the big city." I had moved to the big city and I became a little bit more posh than I was before. I was looking down on everybody. It doesn't matter what you said to me I am not going to pay attention to anyone. Then he said "I have been trying to get to you but you were too rude and difficult" Now he was thinking..... I am getting her because she is pregnant and she has nowhere to go. He said I want to marry you. I told him "I am pregnant" He said "I can marry you and you can go and tell your parents that I am the dad, so I will marry you". For me, I wanted somebody to look after me so I said "OK you can marry me".

He came to my dad and told him he wanted to marry me. My dad was more shocked by this than anything I ever did in my whole life. I was surprised. I was so surprised at why he was shocked. At least I have somebody willing to marry me. You are shocked more than ever so what is wrong with me? Can't I do anything right? I didn't know why my dad was shocked I just didn't know. The whole village was shocked, they said that this girl is too much, she is something else. When the man took me to his house I found out that he already had two wives, and I was the third. On top of all that, this is the man that I saw in prison smoking marijuana more than ten years ago that I was running from. Now Satan has put us together. See how the devil can destroy your life. He will follow you from A to Z trying to see who you are and what you are doing then he will matchmake you with everything that can destroy your destiny. The reason the man, my new husband, was in prison is because he was a killer. He goes around stealing, killing people doing whatever he wants. People were scared of him and couldn't do anything at all about him.

He married me and he went on doing what he did. As long as he was bringing food into my house, I didn't care. I didn't care what he was doing. You think that you have seen bad people in your life? One day he did something, I think he burgled a shop. The owner was powerful like he was so he brought many people and soldiers to come and arrest him. He ran away to another village and he took me with him. My daughter by that time was two years old, and I was five months pregnant with my second child. One month after we were living in the new town, he was arrested for another burglary he committed. Now after his arrest in this town, they told him "We have heard about you, we have heard that you do all these things, that you kill people, but in this town your brother has no power, you are going to die in prison." They said this because he had a brother in the Parliament that used to get him out of prison.

I was a stranger in the city with a two year old girl and 5 months pregnant I was standing in the middle of the street with nothing. My husband was gone to prison, my daughter and I were crying in the streets. We were left with nothing. I had no means to go back to my own village, my own town. I am crying in the street, my daughter is crying daddy, daddy and I am crying, where am I going to go, what am I going to do how can I go back? I cannot walk. It is so far that it would take me days. What am I going to go home to? No family and no friends. While I was crying in the streets, just like that a man passed and looked at me, it turns out that he knew me. He came from the same village as I did. He took me by the hand to his house, got all of his friends together, raised some money and gave it to me for the ticket to go back home.

By this time my mother is already dead, and my father is married to a girl my age. My father is presently in his early 90's, so at that time he must have been in his 50's or 60's and he was married to a woman 18 years old like me. This girl doesn't want to see me in this house. Now my dad is about to give me a second chance, to take me back and this girl has said not in my house. Fortunately, my dad told his wife no, she is my daughter, I'm responsible let her stay.

The day I set foot back in my city the police were waiting for me because of what my husband did. I had to pay for it. While they were waiting for me they were not going to look for me to arrest me. They told my dad he has to take me in to the police. They told him "Don't wait for us to come and get her, because if we do then we are going to arrest you and her, so when she comes back, you bring her to us." I came in the night, and in the morning my dad took me by the hand, and handed me to the police. Now the prosecutor took me into his office. They wanted to hear my side of the story. They wanted me to give a statement and tell what happened. They wanted to know how come I went to my house, was I an accomplice and all that. The prosecutor didn't hear anything I said. At that time I was 6 months pregnant he didn't hear anything, he just raped me and sent me out. He knew that if he didn't do anything but just rape me that I am not going to open my mouth. I'm not going to do anything because he might put me in prison. He just rapes me and takes me out of his office pregnant, 6 months pregnant. Can you imagine? What is happening to the baby that is on the inside of me? The police left me alone because the man raped me. He had nothing that he could do to me anymore, he just left me. From that day I was just looking to take care of the two year old baby that I had, and the pregnancy.

Sometimes you meet a girl that is misbehaving. You don't know what she has been through. You don't know how badly she has been affected. All you do is add curses instead of praying for them. The church has to open its eyes, the Bible says that while the people were sleeping the enemy came and put bad seed, <u>while the people were sleeping</u>. The church is sleeping while the enemy is doing damage to our children to our families. It might not be the children you gave birth to, but she is out there crying and what do you do, look down on her and say "prostitute." Do you care? When they come to the church in their short skirts, what do you do? Tell them to go out and fix themselves and come back. No one can fix themselves, no one. Let somebody come, let Jesus fix them. We know this is a place of worship, we know this is a place of respect, but there are some people who haven't learned that respect yet. Let them in, pray for them and usher them into the presence of God.

They have these big trucks in Congo that are piled high with yams, potatoes, bags of goods and so on. I would climb on top of these big trucks even with my 6 month pregnancy going from place to place looking for men so that I can take care of my baby, so I can take care of my pregnancy. I went on like that until I gave birth to my second daughter. At the time I was giving birth I was already going into bars and drinking and waiting for men. Sometimes you look at people, it doesn't matter how beautiful a prostitute is, it doesn't matter how well dressed they are, deep down on the inside they don't like it. They might pretend before people that they are all that, they might pretend that they like the lifestyle but deep down on the inside they don't like it because no one likes to sleep with different men every day. You want to have intimacy with someone you love, not with anyone who can just give you money and tomorrow they are gone. The reason that I love God the most, the reason I give my all to God is because I could have been HIV positive today, but I am not. God protected me through that. I love Jesus. I am not ashamed at all to give my testimony. It doesn't matter if you put me in the presence of 10,000 people I will say it with no shame because I have been redeemed. I have told God that I will go anywhere he wants me to. No place is too big or too small for me. Sometimes I pay my own money to travel and to win the souls of little girls that are suffering out there because it is not men that are hurting them, but it is Satan.

I started to travel, I start to drink and all these type things. One day I was sitting down in a different city in my country and somebody came and told me you know what, your husband is here and he is looking for you. I said what?" they said "he is out of prison", they let him out by some miracle he did. They said he was going to die in prison. They used to beat him every day. Other people had come also and said he was dead, but by some miracle, what miracle I don't know, he came out of prison and he wanted me back. He didn't go back to his two wives, he left them, he wanted me. For me, I knew already that I didn't want the lifestyle that he was living because he would go to prison again and leave me suffering with babies and everything else I didn't want to go back, but I had no choice. The reason that I had no choice was because I had made a decision that I prefer to be with a killer than sleeping with different men every day. I went back to him. When I went back to him he said that we are going to live in the capital of Congo which is Kinshasa. That is where my whole family has moved to. He wanted me to move there with him. When I went, my family didn't like it at all. You see, sometimes you hear bad news from afar, but when it is at your door, it is too much you don't want it. They said that this girl has brought a lot of shame on our family, we don't want this. Somebody told them, but why don't you give her a second chance. So they gave me a second chance. My sister came and said, if you leave this man we will take you back and give you a second chance. Believe me, it doesn't matter how rude I was, it doesn't matter how stubborn I was on the outside, on the inside I was crying for my family.

I wanted to be close to my family. I wanted my sisters and brothers to like me. I wanted to spend time with them. So I made a decision, I told them yes I'm going to leave the man and I'm coming back. When I came back they got me a place to live and they gave me money to buy and sell second hand clothes. I started doing that. I was going to the market selling clothes and taking care of my children. Deep inside of me, I felt like I was dead there. From the beginning I had no joy. I knew already I wasn't beautiful, therefore it created a little bit of a hole. I had emptiness on the inside of me and I was really trying to fill that hole by doing all sorts of things. That hole, that emptiness was there and there was no peace at all. Every time I was going to the market I was observing the people that were there. I saw two kinds of people plus me, there were three kinds in all. One kind are those who pray so that God can bless them so they can sell well. The other kind is those who can go to the witchdoctor and they do their juju (witchcraft) stuff so they can sell well. The third kind are like me with no devil no God, I was in the middle and now I am looking at myself saying this one is doing well, this one is doing well, I am bound to fail because I don't have anyone to back me up.

I needed to find somebody to back me up because if I fail again, if I lose this money which my sisters have given to me, then they are going to reject me again. I didn't want that to happen. I was so afraid to disappoint them again. I remember that my mother always used to say that I don't go to witchdoctors and I don't want anyone in my family to go to witchdoctors. That is the only thing that I listened to from my mom. I didn't want to make a decision to go to witchdoctors. I said I'm going to learn how to pray.

I didn't know how to pray, every time there would be this desire to learn how to pray to want to pray but I didn't know how to pray. One day I saw a new testament, a blue one called Gideon in my room. I don't know who put it there. I started to read it. While I was reading it, you know the word of God is powerful. The word of God, it doesn't matter where it is, it doesn't matter if you understand it or not. It goes into your spirit and it creates life. That is why I always tell people read your Bible. It doesn't matter if you understand it or not. When we eat food, we don't put it under a microscope and find out how many vitamins A or B are in it we just eat and hope it will do something for our bodies. The same thing is true with the word of God. You don't have to have a revelation every time you read the Bible. You don't have to understand it every time you read it. One thing is for sure, when you read it, it goes in your spirit and it creates life. When I was reading this Bible I didn't understand it at all, I thought that this was the most boring book that I had ever seen. When I reached the part with the psalms, the psalms became like prayers to me because somebody was complaining, somebody was crying, somebody was praising God. I would read the psalms and it would give me a little peace and I would sleep, but there was always something missing.

One day as I am waking up in the morning and I am about to go downtown to buy my clothes to come and sell and I heard a voice say "pray." I turn around and there was nobody. I said "I don't know how to pray." I went again to go out, and the voice went again "pray". I said again, I don't know how to pray. I thought, I know prayers from when I was a child. My mom used to take me to church and there was two prayers that I knew, Hail Mary and Our Father. I thought, OK, let me go and do those prayers and maybe the voice will be satisfied and leave me alone. I went down on my knees and I said Hail Mary even though I didn't know the whole thing. The voice said "no, that is not the prayer that I am looking for." I said Our Father and the voice said "that is not the prayer I am looking for". I am not criticizing the Catholics I am not criticizing their prayers but sometimes we follow routine in the church. Sometimes we tend to do a routine. Today we are going to do this, today we are going to do that. We don't hear what God wants. You can come here in the church, maybe today God doesn't want you to preach, he just wants you to praise him. Because we are used to certain things we get stuck in one place. We have to have this, we have to have that, we have to have the protocol we have to follow. We forget to hear what God wants. You always have to listen to the voice of God.

Now at that time God had a specific prayer that he wanted to hear from me. I believe that he wanted to hear a prayer of repentance. I believe that on that day he wanted me to go on my knees and say "God I am lost I need you". I didn't know how to say that. I knew I was lost but I didn't know how to say that because I was stubborn. I said "You know what, forget it. If that is not the prayer that you want I am out." I went out to the market and the same voice came again "pray" I said "I told you, I don't know how to pray." I came back home that evening and I started to ponder what shall I do, how shall I learn prayer.

I knew that the church could teach you how to pray but I didn't want to go to the church. The reason for this was because I was a bad person. I was always disappointing people and people were always rejecting me. I thought that because I'm bad, because the church is full of good people, if I go to church they will realize or they will notice that I am a bad girl. They are then going to reject me. I've got already my family rejecting me, I don't want the church to reject me also. I will just stay away from them, I didn't want to go to the church.

One day I am just passing from my flat (apartment) to go and visit my sister. I heard people worshiping God. In Kinshasa there are a lot of churches just outside or in somebody's compound. They are always praying and praising God. I have never heard anyone praise God like that before. They were singing and clapping and dancing. When the Bible says God dwells among the praises of His people, that is true. When they are telling you to praise God, it is because God dwells among the praises of his people. You know that when the king comes, even the king of your village, or of Benin, or of Edo state comes in here, he is not just going to come inside and sit down. He is going to ask about your problems. He will say "Now what are your problems, what do you want from me?" You will say "I want money or this or that." If you please him, if you do what he likes he is going to settle your problem. That is what God does, when he comes to dwell he starts to give favors.

When we are praising him, don't do it lightly. You are lifting the King of Kings. You don't know who he is going to draw to himself. The Bible says if we lift the name of Jesus, if we lift Jesus up, He will draw all people unto him. Now, those praises that day drew me to the church. I didn't directly go into the church, I stood there listening. I knew that these people are praising well, they are singing, they are clapping their hands, they must know how to pray. I am going to come back so they can teach me how to pray. After they have taught me how to pray I will just go and pray in my own way and do my own thing. I don't want to come and sit with them.

I went back home, then I started to talk to my neighbor. I said that I was going through this road and I heard people singing and praising, I want to go to that church. I want them to teach me how to praise God. I want them to teach me how to pray. My neighbor said, "Yeah, I will take you. That is my church, I go there." Now listen to this, how many of your neighbors know that you come to the church? I knew my neighbor. We did all sorts, we drank together, abortions, boyfriends, then she would leave me at home on Tuesday and she would go to church. I didn't know she was going to church but we did everything else together. There was no difference between her and I even though she was going to church. There are a lot of people in the church like that. You have to know that whatever you are doing is affecting someone else. People are watching you, they will love God or follow God based on your example. It depends on what you are doing. My neighbor didn't tell me she was going to church until I asked. It was not until I heard the praise and worship, then I told her I wanted to go to church. I don't want to jump ahead of myself but that girl, my neighbor, we are about the same age. Until today she is still in Congo asking for money, doing all sorts, being sick, falling and coming up with nothing. I could even call her my spiritual mom because she is the one that took me to church, but today she has nothing.

Now if you are faithful to God, God will be faithful to you. If you fear God, he will bless you. She took me to church, and when she took me to church, I was sitting down in the very back, paying close attention because this is going to be one shot. I am going to learn to pray today and then just go. I was listening closely. Now I found a man preaching, and he was preaching about the wedding in Cana where they invited Jesus and Jesus turned water into wine. The man was talking about Jesus. He was saying all sorts of things I have never heard before. He was describing the most beautiful handsome powerful Jesus. I have never heard anybody talk like that.

For me, the Jesus that I knew was the Jesus of Christmas. The Jesus where we go once a year to church, then they will show us that Jesus is born in the cradle and then we smile and we are happy. Then we forget about Him. That is the Jesus that I know. The second Jesus that I know is the Jesus where they bring films and they show you Jesus being crucified and people are beating him up and he is bleeding and we are all crying, oh Jesus, oh Jesus. After we finish crying we forget him. That is the Jesus that I knew. He didn't do anything for me. He didn't help me at all. That is not the Jesus that I needed, I needed the Jesus that could put my life back together, I needed the Jesus that was in control. I needed the Jesus that you can call when you are in trouble, I needed the Jesus where you could fall at his feet and say, "Master I'm dying." This Jesus, all he did was just hang on the cross. All he did was get born every Christmas, he was a baby every Christmas. I was tired of this Jesus.

Now this man is describing a new Jesus to me, and that is a revelation. At the back where I was sitting, I was so excited. I wanted to know more about Jesus, and the man was taking his time. You know our preachers, he would tell a story, and he would elaborate on it. I didn't know you could jump in church when the message was too much for you and there is fire and you can jump and say amen. Because I was shy, because I didn't want to draw attention to myself, I was just sitting there saying c'mon, c'mon just tell me quickly about this Jesus. I want to know. I was so hungry. I was so thirsty. The man is just talking and talking. In my mind, I was just thinking that this man that invited Jesus to the wedding is so clever. What I always tell people is that if you want to have a party in Africa, you have to have everything right. You have to have money to buy drinks, you have to have good food. If the party is not a success you are in big trouble, especially a wedding party.

If you are getting married, you put a party on and then your sister doesn't eat, she doesn't drink, she will go home and tell everybody. Now, way after the wedding, when you've got children and grandchildren, they are still talking about the wedding. How it was bad, how they didn't eat, how it was this and that. How the brides clothes were not nice, how she didn't do any shopping in London. The man knew that if he was going to have a good wedding I had better invite Jesus. He knew Jesus was the one who could fix anything, so don't wait for a disaster. Have Jesus in your boat ready to fix any mess that can come in your life. Jesus is mister fix all. He could fix anything, therefore I wanted that Jesus. I had never heard about that Jesus before, I was waiting for that man to tell me how I can have this Jesus. He was saying that you should have this Jesus in your life, your life is a mess, everything is going wrong, you should have this Jesus.

I was thinking yeah, you are talking about me. C'mon, tell me how. I was talking to myself and I was saying c'mon tell me how I can have this Jesus. Finally he said that you have to invite Jesus into your heart so he can be your savior and your master. I was saying to myself, "how do I invite this Jesus". C'mon tell me. In my heart I made a decision that it doesn't matter what they are going to tell me, I am not going out of here without Jesus. Even if I have to drink him like water I am going to drink him. Even if I have to roll on the ground, I am going to roll on the ground, because I want this Jesus. I had enough of my life. Finally he said that those who want to say this prayer come up, and I was the first one. I don't know about anyone else I was the first one. He said say this prayer after me and he told me how to say this prayer, and I prayed the prayer of salvation. Jesus come into my heart be my Savior, forgive my sins.

From that moment, something came into my life. I didn't see lightning, I didn't feel fire, I didn't tremble, I didn't fall, I just knew that everything was going to be alright. From that day, I don't know where it came from but I knew from that moment that everything was going to be alright. I gave my life to Christ. As I was going out, and noticed this, the man in the meeting didn't say that he had a revelation. He didn't say that God is talking to me about someone, that you are a prostitute you are doing all sorts of things, he just said that those who need Jesus come and give your life to Christ. I gave my life to Christ. He didn't name my sin, he didn't tell me to confess my sin. I said forgive me, be my Lord, be my Savior.

I forgot all about the neighbor that brought me to church. I was so happy. For the first time, after I got out of the prayer meeting, I was smiling I was dancing, I was jumping. I think the people who were seeing me around were saying that this girl is crazy. I was jumping around and I was talking to Jesus. I said where have you been all my life? How come you didn't come any sooner? Why did you let me go into all of this trouble just to find you? Anyway, you are here. From now on, no men in my life, I just want you. I made a decision to leave everything behind me. On my way back home I was confessing my sins. Nobody told me to confess my sins. I was telling Jesus everything I was doing and that I am not going to do it anymore. I want to follow you, I want to sing for you, I want to do everything for you. I want to serve you all my life. You are the only man that I want in my life.

Usually when the prayer ends it is about 8:30 or 9 and when there is no electricity it is really dark. When I was going on my way, there was a light around me. I could see it. I don't know if other people could see it, but I saw the light around me. The Bible says He has moved us from the kingdom of darkness to the kingdom of light. I knew that this man Jesus was going to hold me, that this man Jesus was going to help me. I gave my life to Christ and from that day. I just wanted to serve him. Even the decision that I made that I wasn't coming back to church, that I didn't want them to reject me, I forgot about it. The next day I was in the church, every day I was in the church. I was praying I was fasting, I was following God I was reading the Bible. Wisdom came into my life. I started to notice things, I started to realize the things that I was doing that were fruitless, things that didn't help me at all. As a result my family took me back completely.

When I gave my life to Christ, this is what you have to realize, everything doesn't go from wrong to right overnight. It takes time, it takes dedication it takes effort in God when you give your life to Christ. Don't think you are going straight to heaven. You still have the same things to battle against, you still have the devil to fight. You still have to make that decision every day. You live everyday life to say I am going to serve my master.

My family, they are very secular, they drink like crazy. There is one member of my family that doesn't eat a meal without a beer. They do all kinds of things and they don't care about it. They go to church, but when they come back they do the same things. I made a decision that I am going to follow Christ. When I was suffering I was suffering alone, my friends mocked me, my family turned their backs on me, I had no one. When I made my decision, I didn't look who is serving God and who is not when I was coming in the church. I didn't look at who is fearing God, and who is not. When I came to church I didn't care who is reading the Bible and who is playing. Who is serious and who is not. When I came to the church, I didn't care if the pastor was serious or not. I looked at Christ and Christ alone. He is the one who gave his life for me. There were pastors around when I was suffering there were sisters around when I was suffering. Now that I met Jesus, I am not going to pay attention to what people are doing wrong. I'm not going to be offended because people danced the wrong way or maybe they kicked me a little bit. Someone can say something and then people will storm out of the church. They say "I am not coming back" maybe they are not desperate enough, for me I had nowhere else to go, I had no one, I had only Christ.

People sometimes ask me " How come you serve God this way, how come you go around doing this and exposing your life" If God has took you from Hell, and brought you back, believe me you will love Him. I was so desperate that I followed God with all my heart. Sometimes nowadays you tell people we have a revival, when they are invited they will say "I don't have a ticket, I don't have any money for transportation, I can't go there it is too far." I used to walk miles to come to church because I didn't have any ticket or transportation money. I walked to church and I walked back home.

Now, my family was saying that they wanted me to be a good person. I became a good person and the reason that I became a good person was because of Jesus. Now they turned around and said that they don't want this Jesus thing. They said "You pray too much, you fast too much you are skinny like you're going to die because of the fasting, because of the prayer, we don't want this". I told them make a choice, it is simple; without Christ I cannot be a good person. Do you want the old Edo back, or the new one with Christ? People are going to give you an ultimatum they are going to force you to make a choice of what you want.

Sometimes we say "I don't want to lose friends so you leave Christ, you want to follow your friends. Now these friends are going to abandon you when you are in trouble. For me, I knew that the best friend that I had was Christ. I had made a decision to stick with Him, and I was serious about it. I was in it every day. They used to give us lessons about how to pray, how to read your Bible, it was like a Sunday school where they would teach you so many things, how to preach to others. Every time they would give me one lesson, I would take it and give it to someone else. That is how I learned how to preach. If you would teach me on Sunday this is how to pray, this is how to ask for forgiveness, then I would find someone else to teach what I had been taught. I was doing Gods' work. I was following people who were already mature in faith. I was following them everywhere. If they were going to the hospital to visit the sick I was behind them. If they were going to the orphanages, I'm behind them. If they are going to the prisons to preach the word I'm behind them. I was not preaching, I was just observing what they were doing. This was not in vain, nothing you do for God is wasted, nothing. The time you give to God is a seed. The words, the prayers that you send to God is a seed, one day you will reap it. It might take longer but you will reap it.

Now as I was praying, as I was serving God as I was going around trying to learn everything I found myself right in the middle of everything that had to do with Jesus. It was the 80s, at that time the revival came among students. Most of the people who were among us were students, bright, clever, intellectual people. Here was this little girl who just finished secondary school and doesn't know anything. That doesn't intimidate me. I don't care if you are from the university, I am here for Christ. I'm just observing. I just want to learn from you. I didn't hide, I didn't go and say that these people are too clever for me. When you are following Christ, nothing matters. Nothing matters, whether you have clothes or you don't have clothes you still follow God. I say that because at that time I didn't have even have clothes or shoes to take to church. I was coming to church every day. People came well dressed, they had nice clothes, they had jewelry and everything. I didn't have any. Praise God, I came as I was. I was washing my knickers overnight, washing and hanging so tomorrow I could wear them. I was washing my skirt overnight so tomorrow I could go to church. I didn't use the excuse that because I didn't have clothes I am not going. One thing I learned, one verse that was building me up. The Bible says seek first the kingdom of God and his righteousness and all of these things shall be added unto you.

I followed the kingdom, I chased the kingdom, I served the kingdom, I loved the kingdom, I lived the kingdom, I slept the kingdom, I woke up the kingdom. I didn't give up. Everything that was to be done in the kingdom, I was doing it. If they said to sing I was singing, if they said to set up the chairs, I was setting them up. If they said to sweep, I was sweeping. If the church was starting at 5 o'clock, four I was there. If somebody needed prayer I was praying for them. If somebody needed some study lesson I would give it to them until prayer started, then I would sit down and pray and then go home. Now at this time I'm not worried. Never. This is the truth, God as my witness. Never. Even though we were fasting 21 days, we fasted for 40 days, for 3 days without food without water. Never in my life did I put my knees down and say God give me food, God give me a husband. Never, because that was the least of my worries. I wasn't worried about these things anymore. My worry was for the kingdom of God to go forward. I was doing that all the time. I was preaching and teaching and doing everything I could.

One day my brother that was in London heard that my sister had lost her husband. He said "I know my sister is going to have a hard time. I want her to come and rest a little bit in London." My sister had two children, plus she took my children also. I didn't have anywhere to put the children, plus the pressure of school, so she was taking care of my children too. She was raising 4 children two of mine and two of hers.

When she wanted to go to London, she took my children too because she didn't want to divide them. The children were already together all the time. Two of the children became like twins. She didn't want to leave them, so she took them all to London with her. Now when she was in London, you know how hard it is in Europe, it is so hard to raise children. You have to go everywhere with them. When you leave them alone in the house, the social services will move in, the police will move in and they will take the children away. My sister was not used to taking care of the children by herself. She always had a helper around. Now she found herself in Europe raising four children. It became too much so she became depressed. Now my brother said "let's call somebody to come and help you look after the children". Guess who my sister said to call? Do you think it was me? No, it was the house girl in Congo.

They got the passport and everything ready for the house girl to come to London. When they went to get the visa, they found out the house girl was pregnant. Because she was pregnant, that meant that if she came to London, she was bringing more work with her than they thought. Since they didn't have any other choice, they brought me to London. So, even when you are not looking for it, and you are not praying for it, God has a plan and he can work it out in your life. Gods plan was for me to come to London. I eventually learned English and became a UK citizen.

I wasn't looking to come to UK, I was looking to be faithful. God had a plan for his will to come forth, even thought I didn't see it at the time.

Because of what God was doing in my life, I wanted to go back to tell my people what he was doing in my life. The verse that He gave me was about the madmen in the tombs who was set free. He wanted to be with Jesus. Jesus told him that you have to go to your people and tell them what God has done for you. That is how God put it on my heart to do a revival in Congo.

What I did to get what I needed from God in order to do the revival was to pray and get in Gods' presence. I didn't know anyone, and I wasn't known. If there was a conference, I would go, if there was a revival I would go. I wanted his presence more than anything else.

Every penny I made was for the revival. I didn't buy any luxuries for myself, no house, no expensive clothes nothing like that. After about three years I had saved up enough money. During this time I also started a Bible study in my house ministering to young people. The study grew from about 5 to over 45 people. I didn't take money from the children because they were college age and they really didn't have any.

I had saved enough money for the revival, and like I said I was always going to revivals to be in God's presence. One night I was watching God TV and saw the Lakeland Florida revival. Since I had been sending the money for the revival to Congo, I didn't have the money to go to Lakeland. Since Todd kept saying come and get some, I decided to come and get some. My daughter Clarice gave me the money for the airfare to come to Lakeland, but I still didn't have the money for a hotel room. The children at the Bible Study wanted me to come, so they raised the money to pay for my hotel.

I came to Lakeland in May 2008. My first night, as soon as I arrived I changed and went straight to the revival. The first night was a little strange for me. I didn't know anyone, I felt lonely, I didn't feel anything. I was thinking it was better to watch the revival at home on my TV. This was because I could keep an eye on my responsibilities, and worship in my own home. After I went back to the hotel the power of God hit me. It happened like this, I wanted to watch TV because I didn't feel anything and I was even regretting that I came. When I went to turn on the TV I felt God say "don't". I then started to feel the power of God hovering over me, it was as if there was the sound of a wind over me. Then the room filled with this heat and I felt so hot. I knew that it was the presence of God. That presence started dealing with everything, the loneliness, the pain I was feeling, and the problems I was having.

The second day I was there, I went to Ignited Church in the morning, and then again that evening. That evening I arrived about 4 pm and I was allowed in early, which was a courtesy extended to pastors that were coming from afar.

While I was sitting there, a man asked me if anyone was sitting next to me, and I said no. It turned out that he was a man named Andrew Snyder. It was nice to have someone to talk to. After the program, I asked him if I could borrow his phone. He asked me who I needed to call, and I said that I wanted to call a taxi to take me to my hotel. He said he could give me a lift. As a woman I don't recommend taking lifts from people you just met. This was especially so for me because I was a stranger in another land. No one knows I am here and anything could happen. I didn't feel any fear, the thought of other possibilities slipped my mind and I said yes. Andrew dropped me at my hotel and over the next week we began a friendship that continues to this day.

This is my story in my own words, and that is how I met Andrew. The rest of the book tells of our adventure together in Congo.

The Beginning

MY name is Andrew Snyder. I am was born and raised in the midwest of the United States of America. I am divorced, in my mid forties, and a college educated Caucasian. I didn't always believe in Jesus. Actually I thought that people that followed Him were idiots. Looking back now, I realize that I thought a lot of foolish, stupid and immature things. This was because I was thinking with my natural mind. It was really quite similar to a scientific approach. I looked at the available evidence, then formed an hypothesis. I looked at how people lived their daily lives that went to church, I looked at the evil done in the name of God world wide, I looked at news stories that covered Christian events in the news, I looked at the human suffering. How could a good God allow all of this suffering?, I asked. Based on the evidence I had seen so far I reasoned with my natural mind and then completely discounted the possibility that God even existed. I felt the demonic attacks and the guilt of sin but I just thought that it was normal in life. Is that a case of simple mindedness, or deception of the enemy or both? I was a godless man in a godless world. Well, the devil is a liar, and I had no idea that I was buying one of his lies.

I was approached in college, "We are having a Bible study, would you like to come?" well, I had no intention of wasting my time with that activity. The man who asked me was nice enough, and persistent. I kept politely declining, and then probably not so nicely. I mean really, what about all the different religions? If God is so great and all that why can't His followers get it together? I was told that this was the purpose of the Bible study, to look into questions like that. Bible study wasn't the popular thing to be doing at a state university, especially when there was so much partying to attend to. The Bible thumpers took a lot of heat from the rest of the dorm residents about their beliefs because they were different, clean cut, polite, sober minded. To be seen talking to them or to be seen going to the Bible study was surely going to invite ridicule.

I'm not sure what was the final ingredient that got me to the Bible study, the gentle persistence, that they seemed to walk in peace even though in that environment of verbal and social persecution, it shouldn't really have been happening. Eventually I went to the Bible study, and then to church. I felt really out of place and awkward. There was something wrong, they had peace and happiness, joy and a spirit about them. What it was I didn't know but I determined to get to the bottom of it all. I was given a new testament and read it in order to disprove it. I had always heard that the Bible was full of holes and misinterpretations. OK, so I was an idiot. Everyone should read the Bible for themselves, the world would be a better place. It is hard to admit you are wrong, but God allows it and has more than ample grace and forgiveness for the sins committed in ignorance. He even forgives us for willful ignorance. It is funny really, how we can be so dull of hearing and so ignorant once you see it for yourself. We all have tests and trials that we have to go through in life, you can ignore the obvious if you want to, I did it many times because I was not ready to wrap my head around the realities that are now so obvious.

Through this life we are really on a path of revelation, God is revealing more and more of Himself to us as we go along and as we become ready to absorb it. We willfully ignore reality because we have our personal schedules and goals, and we are not ready to let go of our personal beliefs, goals and schedules in order to allow the Lord to do with us what He wants. He doesn't force us to have all the best, you are free to do it the hard way. I just finally got to the point where I was ready, it took a lot but He took me there. Its so much better. I just couldn't see it with my natural mind.

Once I realized the truth, inside myself, in my inner man I sincerely wanted to live in a manner pleasing to God. I didn't want to be self deceived like the religious people in Jesus' day. I really wanted to walk it out perfectly so God would be pleased. Unfortunately, I was trying to do it by my own strength and ability. This thought is a little bit advanced, and is therefore difficult to explain. It is like this…It is not possible for man to please God on our own because we don't have it in ourselves to do so. If we did, then Jesus wouldn't have had to come to this earth and die for us. However, that does not mean that we can live any way we want to. We are to grow to the point where we walk in the Spirit of God all the time. We can get to the point where the things of this earth are no longer interesting, so we are no longer tempted by them. It starts on the inside, and works its way to the outside, not the other way around.

I didn't know it, but I started in rituals and religion. I had a zeal for the things of God, and made every effort to do right. Without realizing it I was walking in the traditions of men. Jesus said, "whom the Son sets free is free indeed." I didn't know. I learned to be a Christian in the natural, physical realm. Follow the rules, do this and that. Walking in my own understanding, and doing it by self discipline, and in my own strength. God is above the natural world. It is impossible to do what God has called us to do in the physical, natural realm. Jesus said, "Apart from Him (referring to God) I can do nothing" Who are we to think that it would be possible to do the things God has told us to do by our own strength, when Jesus couldn't do it? You may have to experience it for yourself before you can fully understand what I am saying. I know I had to get the revelation that way. It was a big revelation for me, and it took a while to grasp it. Until I understood, I did a lot in the natural. I studied and read the Bible, did the stuff I was told, and repeated and taught others as well.

I did evangelism in the natural, it was like being a salesman. You divide the city in quadrants, break it down to the street level, and make assignments. Legalism steps in along with the quotas and the pressure. I mean its OK, after all the work was supposedly for the Lord, it was just not His way. If you make enough calls, eventually someone buys your product. Evangelism became a numbers game. Things are done by goal setting, performance reviews, learning your product and sharing it with others. God used the effort for His good purpose, it just wasn't the best way.

When you get beyond the natural, and Jesus becomes a relationship, then we go to Him about our day, and He shares what we need to be about. There is a whole deeper discussion that I would like to present, You may understand immediately, and then it could take days to get you to believe and understand. Briefly, we are sons as Jesus was a Son. Jesus heard from the Father, and we are to be like Him. It is available for us, but the people in religion don't yet walk in it, so they don't want you to walk in it either, because it makes them look bad. The tendency of religious people is to misunderstand or misinterpret the scriptures in order to explain what isn't happening in their lives. I hope you are still reading because this is the teaching that many Christians aren't ready for. They are still saved, it is just that they are missing out on so much. I want you to see it, so let down your walls, relax your mind, and allow the Lord to show you what He wants you to see.

Religion is like pressure, don't do this, don't do that, rules, legalism, acting correctly. Freedom is much better. I mean, try to walk in it, but don't be so uptight. God Loves us and He knows we are going to mess it up from time to time.. Peter didn't walk it out perfectly and he was with the Lord every day. The Lord doesn't expect us to do it in our strength, rather we are to do it in His. Trust me, it is a much happier, easier, and fulfilling experience. If you are trying to teach your children something do you take them and tan their backsides the first time they do it wrong? No, we understand that they are learning, and we give them the grace to make mistakes while they learn. Of course we expect them to move forward and quit making the same "mistakes" forever.

I dropped the ball a few times. Seriously. I got frustrated and grew quite cold. The devil is a liar. His game is to wear the Lord's people down mentally and discourage them. The devil has lies that he tells us. These lies may attack the leadership for their shortcomings, or they attack the people by telling us that the believers are all hypocrites. The game is always the same. The devil tries to wear us down mentally because there are things that are not correct according to how we *think* things should be in our hypercritical minds. We think things like "brother so and so didn't treat me right, so I am leaving the church" I have been mistreated severely by people, but I finally realized that it was the devil trying to break me. The Lord is my strength. A strong and mighty tower. Those who run to Him are safe. I didn't understand the spiritual battle we are in. The devil and his people hate us, they want to kill us any way they can. God has his protection around us, and we are safe in Him and in Him alone.

The Lord was faithful, he drew me back into His will. He broke the things of the world and the things of religion off of me and set me free. He is in the process of doing it for you as well. It is both easy and difficult to grasp this concept. That is because the natural man cannot understand the things of the Spirit because they are spiritually discerned. In other words, the natural man really doesn't have the skill set. If you are not tracking with me, it is OK, hang around a little and you will see it. The early Apostles didn't get it either, that is why Jesus had to explain the parables to them. It is not about being a better person or a stronger believer, or addressing another shortcoming in your life. Things of the Spirit are not about beating yourself up over our faults and weaknesses. In the Spirit we are growing in the depth of our understanding. This growth is a gift, and God gives liberally to all men. I'm not going to elaborate on my struggles, lack of spiritual insight, shortcomings, and falls because they don't add much to the story, and they are in the past and they are difficult to relive. It is best to let that stuff go, don't beat yourself up, and trust that the Father. He has ample grace for us as He transforms us into the likeness of His Son.

My major troubles actually began in November of 2002. I had a successful business that was doing around $750,000 in annual sales. I had the rest of the package too. I had a large home on a large lot overlooking a beautiful river that was over a mile wide. I had a wonderful wife and son. Everything looked like it was going well, but the reality proved to be different. I was serving the Lord in the best way I knew how in the natural. The business grew until it took all of my time. Family life began to suffer. The accuser of the brethren was on his job, verbally attacking the weak spots and starting vile rumors. The details of the experience would fill another book. The bottom line was that the things that were important to me were suddenly gone, along with a substantial personal fortune. It is out of our weakness and suffering that The Lord can most use us. When we are at the point that we realize we cannot go on. When the task is beyond our ability, then He gets the glory.

Ultimately, the Lord drew me into a new relationship with Him where I had to unlearn all of the bad mindsets that I had been taught. It was a relationship where He ruled supreme as the centerpiece of my life. Before I could go where He wanted me to go, I had to go through a crushing process, a breaking process like the clay on the potters wheel. It was not until He was satisfied, and I had learned what He wanted me to know: that obedience is the best way. Wait on Him, listen for the still small voice. I am not saying that the Lord took away my things, or that He did these things to me, I am saying that in my stubbornness, my disobedience and my self willfulness I brought these things upon myself. I thought I was following Him closely, but later I learned that I was following Him my way, according to my own understanding.

So, for the next few years, I was getting equipped and healed for the next segment of the journey that lay ahead. This was done through a serious devotion to the Lord and to His work. I was in a good church where the leadership understood getting in the presence of God, and equipping the saints. We always had wonderful guest speakers. The people were very devoted, and they "got it". Church wasn't a social club, it was a hospital for the broken.

The Revival

THE church that I attended in Sarasota, Florida was very different from a traditional "religious" setting. The pastor refused to run a schedule Sunday morning, or any time for that matter. We started worship around 11:30 or 11:45 depending on the day. We even had worship as early as 10 am if you wanted to worship while the worship team warmed up. This could often be the best time all day, because some of the people hadn't come in yet carrying their burdens from the week before. There was no set order for the songs, or how long the worship service lasted, or how long the preaching went. On some days, the service would run until 2:30pm, other times it went until 4 or 4:30pm. It all depended on what the Holy Spirit wanted to do. It was all very interesting and different.

The pastor was also very prophetic. One time a woman came to church, but none of us knew who she was. The service was running longer than usual. People always showed up when they could, and left at various times towards the end of the service. Actually, it was all quite casual. Towards the end of the service, the lady was leaving, but it was still during the service. The pastor stopped preaching, and told her to wait because the Lord had a word for her. The pastor then said that he saw a legal battle all around her, and the woman began to weep a little. Then the pastor said "You are going to be victorious, you are going to get custody of your children" Well, the woman lost it right there, and just cried her eyes out. We all knew the Pastor had heard the Lord, and the Lord had just told her what she needed to hear.

Another time the pastor said "Who is going to the doctor in the next few days" He said it three times. Finally a Hispanic woman came forward to be prayed for. She was nervous because she didn't speak much English. I think that was also a factor in why she didn't come forward for prayer right away, because she might not have understood what he was saying. I was one of the "catchers" that had to try and catch people if they fell over from Gods presence during prayer. (I didn't believe in all this when I started, I felt it was an act, but after catching a few people that were out cold, I realized I was wrong.) When we prayed for her, the power of God was very strong, and I felt it whoosh through me even though I was several feet away. We all knew she was healed. It was an impression, I just knew she was healed, but I didn't know what of. Several weeks later she came back to testify that she had had Hepatitis C and that the doctors had tested her again twice (to be sure) and it was completely gone. From what I understand, Hepatitis C is an incurable blood condition that will eventually end in death. It was no longer there, so the only explanation is that God wanted to step in and supernaturally remove that curse from her.

Not only was the worship very nice, and the preaching good, and the prophetic flowing, and God was doing miracles signs and wonders, but the pastor didn't "own" the pulpit. There were many other members that were encouraged to preach, teach and share revelations that the Lord was giving them. We had many guest speakers, most of which were very gifted speakers, they stayed scripturally accurate, flowed in the prophetic, and miracles signs and wonders followed. One guy tried to get people to follow him away, and another was real tricky, extracting money from the congregation, but the majority of the speakers were wonderful.

We also went to see other speakers when they were in the area, sometimes traveling hundreds of miles to do so. One of the speakers that we saw during all of this was an evangelist named Todd Bentley. *(OK, those of you who know Todd, or know of Todd, watch your mouth right now in Jesus name. God used Todd in an amazing way, and the Lord isn't done with him either. I know Todd's went through a rough period, but God still used Todd. Instead of stoning our wounded, intercede for him. Repeat after me "Lord, thank you for using Todd in a mighty way, Lord we ask that you will reach out to Todd in a special way and touch him as only you can. Satan we come against you and your attacks in our lives and in Todd's life, in Jesus name amen")*

God used Todd in an amazing way. Todd usually called people out of the audience by where they were sitting and by their medical conditions. He even usually had several other details about their lives. Then he would pray for them, and they would be healed. The teaching was especially deep and insightful. Todd was wild too, he was covered with tattoos, wore jeans and a t-shirt, had an ear ring, and basically drove the conservative religious folks nuts, because they couldn't grasp how God could use a man that looked like that. I guess they couldn't understand that it wasn't the man, it was what was in the man that allowed him to move in God like that. We all know the saying "Don't judge a book by it's cover" and we should be familiar with the saying " God sees not as a man sees for man looks at the outward appearance, but God looks at the heart." The religious leaders want everyone to conform to their rules and regulations because that is a demonstration of their power over the lives of the people. It is also an attempt to clean the outside of the cup without dealing with the real issues. Who was it that were experts at that...the Pharisees? There is more strict legalism in the church than there should be, and the people are sick of it. The church is a hospital, and the leaders are supposed to help people out of bondage, and that is not done by exchanging one form of bondage for another. Todd did a good job of being on target and dealing with issues and teaching things that others wouldn't touch. Say what you will now, at that time we didn't know where this was all headed. Additionally, people need to realize that the Lord isn't done with Todd either.

Todd Bentley came to Lakeland Florida on April 2nd 2008 for a 5 day conference. I liked Todd's style and I went there from the first night when less than 500 people were there, and I basically caught every night from then until I left for Africa. I missed 4 or 5 nights completely and a few I caught on God TV, so I wasn't there in person. Essentially, I either drove back and forth from Venice, Florida, to Lakeland, or I stayed there in

Lakeland for the next 90 days. In the very beginning, the presence of God was so strong you could almost cut it with a knife. People were so happy, loving and caring. It was great. One of the first nights the auditorium at Ignited Church smelled like smoke. The smoke smelled like burning wood mixed with frankincense. There was no fire, just the presence of the Lord manifested in a smell. Unusual? You bet. It is hard to explain in words, you really just had to be there. The first day or two I realized that the revival that was going to break out was going to fill stadiums and spread to other cities and other stadiums around the world. The Lord was showing me what He was going to do before it happened.

Well, the revival got huge. It blew up to over 10,000 people a night from all over the world. There were hundreds of miracles every night. I had never seen anything like it in my life. Since this book is not about dissecting the revival, I am just skimming the highlights. The revival moved several times because no one realized what God was doing until it happened. It first went to a church in Auberndale, Fl. then to a baseball stadium, to the Lakeland center, to the airport, and then back to the Lakeland center, then back to the airport in a tent so big it would have almost fit a 747 in it.

One day, a day which was a very fateful day for me, I was at Ignited Church during the revival. I think it was for the evening service. I was late, because I had to work. By the time I arrived, there were almost no vacant seats at all. Every day, hundreds of people would stand outside of Ignited Church for hours and then save seats for their friends that had not yet arrived. There were empty seats that were saved for people that were going to arrive late. At other times people would get up and walk around so a seat would appear vacant. In order to get a seat in the auditorium, I had to work the crowd. If I did not find a seat, I would be stuck in the overflow room watching on the big TV screen. I began asking people with empty seats next to them if the seat was taken. I worked my way through about half the people in the auditorium. One seat was available next to a black lady, so I asked if the seat was taken. She said no, so I sat down. Her "no" was unusual, because the accent was not one I could pin down. I asked where she was from. The answer was "London" well, that didn't fit either. After a short discussion I discovered that I was sitting next to Edo Mukeza, and that she was an evangelist that was born in the Democratic Republic of the Congo (Kinshasa). After the revival was over for the evening, Edo asked me to borrow my telephone so that she could call a cab to take her back to the hotel. Since her hotel was near mine, and I had a car, I offered to take her to her hotel so that she could save the cab fare. She accepted, and we made arrangements for transportation in the morning as well. So, on it went for the week she was there. I served the revival by providing transportation. It was not the first time I had made international connections, nor was it the first time that I had been a "taxi driver" for the revival. It is important to serve others.

Edo told me that she was planning to go to the Congo in July to speak at several churches. She had been there the year previous, and had been well received. Several of the churches in Congo had come together this year and they were planning a city wide revival. In addition to that, the crowd was expected to be 6,000 souls. The estimate went as high as 30,000 souls, but that proved to be high. The Congo is a difficult and very foreign place. I really wanted to go the second I first heard of it because it sounded like a good adventure. There are always considerations. I didn't want to be a burden or in the way. I knew that if I went, Edo and I were going to be in close contact for weeks, and during difficult travel people can really grate on each other. This is of course true for Christians as well, because we are still people.

The biggest consideration of them all was...did the Lord want me to go. If I am doing something because of improper motives such as impressing others, or just for the fun of it then He would not bless the work. Additionally, it could be very dangerous to be there without His covering and blessing. I sought the Lord, so that I could have peace about it. I also spent some time getting to know Edo so we could be comfortable together. There was one other difficulty that had to be addressed.

When men and women are together, there can be romance. So, we had to be comfortable together, but not too comfortable. The work of the Lord cannot be done in the flesh, His work is purely supernatural. He can only move in vessels that are clean, so being on a mission field and slipping into sin would be very disastrous for us as well as for the goals of the trip. After some time we got used to one another. It was apparent from the beginning that we both understood the relationship.

Edo was in Lakeland for a week, and we became close in the Lord. She had actually come to Lakeland in order to get in Gods presence and to seek His face about the revival. I think she had also hoped to get some support from the believers at the revival. Support didn't have to be just financial. 6,000 people is a lot of people to minister to on any given night. There is a corporate anointing as well. The Lord sent the disciples out by twos, they were stronger together because they could be encouraged by each others faith. The Bible also says "Let every matter be established by two or more witnesses" If there were more strong Christians there, then there would be a stronger anointing and we could mutually strengthen and encourage each other. There would be more active giftings as well. Like watchmen on the wall, we could do shifts, thereby keeping everyone sharp and fresh.

I don't think Edo's search for support went the way she thought it would. It is easy to imagine in the natural that the Lord would send you to a revival, and that when you arrive, that the leaders of that revival would welcome you with open arms once they discovered that you were doing a revival also. Americans are funny. I cannot speak about other cultures because I do not really know them well enough. Americans love the brand. We are suckers really. Everyone is doing it so it must be right. We want to be in the "in" club. Seriously. My business had better product than my competition, but because I didn't have brand name recognition, my sales suffered. As Christians we want to support famous ministries, even though they may have grown to the point where they are no longer walking in what they started with. We love the brand, and we love to name drop. It gives us a comfort, but it is based on the natural, rather than on what the Lord is saying. My point is that if you are unknown, then it is more difficult to get support. I realize people could be thinking that scoundrels could run off with the money, the leadership could disappoint, and so on. We are thinking in the natural. We should be asking "what does the Lord say about this" We are really face receiving aren't we....like James addresses in the Bible.

As churches, we seldom work together. There is a competition, the church across town is winning more people, and they are stealing disciples. Don't worry about that. Teach your people to listen to the Lord, then they will go where He directs. If they are leaving your ministry, check with the Lord and see what His purpose is. Bees leave the hive as a swarm because it is a natural thing, it creates expansion and growth. Bees also leave if there is danger. If the enemy is attacking, and the disciples don't know how to fight, then they will flee instead of defeating the adversary. Revivals aren't much different than churches. Men want to own and control them. They can be very lucrative, and the money can become the motivation. Jesus didn't die so you could have a new Cadillac every year.

Revivals are not ours to own, they are ours to serve, they are ours to pray about, we need to keep seeking the Lord in order to be aware of the hidden dangers. Due to the fact that Edo was unknown in the US, yet famous in the Congo, the revival in Lakeland didn't receive her like they would have if they had known her. Its OK, the Lord had a better plan, and we were looking to Him anyway as our provider and our King. If we do everything in the natural, then it is not possible for the Lord to get the Glory. The natural mind can see the way the revival could support this work, and for some, that is what happens. These people are probably the people that supported the work years ago, people who believed when it didn't look possible and worked diligently for years. Now they are enjoying the fruit of their labor. Why should they open their checkbooks to finance what the Lord has told us to do, when they need the funds to do what the Lord has told them to do? We have to look past the natural and realize that the Lord has it all figured out already, all we have to do is follow Him.

The Lord answered Edo's prayers, but in a different package. Not the strong and the well known, but the weak and the broken. In spite of the apparent shortcoming to the natural mind, it turned out to be exactly what the Lord wanted. "My strength is made perfect in weakness" As it turned out, we were pretty close to the same level in the Lord, and with giftings that complemented each other. The Lord doesn't come in the package we would like. We judge by the outward appearance, and the Lord looks at the heart. We need to be mature and realize that the word of the Lord can come from any source He desires. Remember, He even spoke to the prophet Baalam through a donkey.

During the time that Edo and I were together in Lakeland, she invited me to come to London. I had never been there, and at the very least it was a chance to see part of Europe. Additionally, I would be able to get to know her better, and see the work that she was doing with the young men and women in London. I went to London for a week, saw the sights, met her children. Met the children at the Bible study and set up the plans for the revival.

After I was in London, Edo decided to come to Lakeland again in order to marinate in Gods presence some more, and to get charged up for the work of the Lord. This time we stayed in the same hotel. (In separate rooms.) I knew by this time that I was definitely going to the Congo, but I had not yet purchased my ticket. God has an interesting way of working things out.

On the night of June 14th 2008 at the revival, Todd dedicated quite a bit of time to the work they were doing in Darfur. Now Darfur is a real mess. People dying of starvation, the whole bit. The work was admirable, rescuing child soldiers and teaching them about Jesus. They showed a short movie, and Todd raised something like $250,000 in an hour or so. He also called for volunteers to go to Darfur and help with the food distribution. They needed 120 volunteers, so I volunteered. It sounded really cool to be serving the people in Darfur, seeing the signs and wonders close up, and working with Todd. I downloaded the application form and purposed to help. One of my strengths is in satellite and data communications, therefore I know how to install high speed data satellite equipment for remote internet access. I was thinking that we could broadcast the work in Darfur over the internet. I called and emailed Fresh Fire Ministries multiple times without getting a response. I am sure that they were just swamped because of the revival. I wanted to talk to someone because I didn't just want to go as a tourist. I wanted to be active in the ministry. There are people who want to be able to brag that they went somewhere interesting with a famous evangelist, and that is one of their primary considerations.

I was more interested in working and serving. I never did get in touch with anyone at Fresh Fire with any more authority than the girl that answered the phone. That fact, coupled with the $4,000 price tag caused me to hesitate long enough for me to meet Edo and to realize that this is where I was needed. It turned out for the best because I don't think Todd ever went to Darfur, and I don't know what happened to the people that went there, but I am sure that the experience was anticlimactic.

On to the Congo - The Chronicles

THE following is a copy of the notes that I took in the Congo while on the trip. For the most part, this section is a word for word copy of what I wrote when I was in the Congo. Because I didn't have a laptop in Congo, I wrote all of this in a small notebook and then transcribed it later into a computer. I fixed the spelling and grammar as needed. Some parts were incomplete and somewhat disjointed as well. Sometimes I just had to leave them that way. Any additional comments or any part of the story that I felt needed to be elaborated upon, were added in *italics*. This section really retains a great deal of the flavor of the experience. Sometimes the events drag out very slowly, other times it is extremely fast paced and interesting. I felt that it was important to the integrity of the story to report all of the events that I could exactly as I recalled them, rather than just the exciting highlights. In this way, I will also be able to give you a better feel for the experience as you read.

5-28-08 I am at the Lakeland Florida, home of the 2008 revival. I was in my hotel room worshiping the Lord and preparing to go to the revival for the evening. I saw myself in a vision. In the vision I was on a small hill 1 to 2 feet high with a gentle slope away in all directions. Here and there were some small pine trees in the distance. It looked like there was snow on the ground that was around 8-12" deep. Upon closer examination, I realized that the snow was actually diamonds, brilliant white diamonds sparkling in the sun. (pv 31:10, rev 12:4) Later I saw a grey cat with white paws and a white spot on his chest, like grey cats get. I couldn't actually see the paws because he was big and fluffy and the paws were tucked under his body, like cats do. I just knew they were white. He was sitting on a dark blue quilted pillow by a window, looking out of the window. The cat was quite contented, perhaps he was looking at the diamonds.

6-1-08 I was at Victory Christian Church where I had another vision. I saw a big round rock, then behind it, many smaller rocks that formed a stream bed. The rocks were covered with a light snow, and a cold clear stream was running through the rocks and down the stream bed. I felt that the large rock was the rock of ages, and the cool stream water was the refreshening for those that thirst.

7-3-08 I know that I'm going to the Democratic Republic of the Congo. The Lord has been giving me visions or mental pictures of what it is going to be like there.

7-04-08 The journey has been a little strange. I didn't understand that dreams and visions could even be from the Lord. I felt that even if they were, then it was for someone more spiritual than myself. I thought that I would buy a notebook and write down the visions that I have as they come to me. I have had some limited feelings or impressions in the past. For instance, I was on vacation in Costa Rica. There was a woman in her 20's there at the hot springs. I got a strong feeling or impression she was from Michigan, so I asked her if she was from Michigan. It was out of the blue, and she seemed a little surprised. Then I said, let me see if I can get the city. Then I felt like she was from Ann Arbor, so I said "Are you from Ann Arbor?" She got a little concerned or frightened and said "what, are you a psychic or something?" I said no, but I didn't understand the point of it, I didn't know what that was about, or where it was coming from.

After a few of these experiences in Lakeland, I felt I needed to get a notebook to write all this down so I didn't forget. Quite a few weeks after I got the vision of the snow that was actually diamonds, I realized that the Congo is actually a major producer of diamonds. With Congo, I am feeling like the problem is that the people won't work in unity and deal with national sins. Therefore they are not being blessed, although the resources are there for them, but it is not a vision it is more like a mental impression.

When we went to London, Edo and I travelled to New Castle England so she could speak in a church. Before we left I got a vision of castles, deep dark staircases and medieval gates that related to the gates and demonic strongholds and ancient curses brought on the land by Pagan, Wiccan and Druid practices.

7-08-08 I had to remember to write the vision of the rose and the volcano. I don't have time to write it now, but I wanted to remind myself to write it. *I never did write it, but now I have forgotten the details. Essentially I saw a volcano erupting and then a rose budding. I believe the volcano represents a sudden explosion of the gospel and the rose represents the rose of sharon, that is Christ.*

Last night a seed pod popped into my mind while in prayer. It looked like a nut with a rind on it. It divided into four parts and was about the size of a walnut. Then I saw something else, but I need to remember it. I am going to move my book so I can write these thing as I go.

Tonight, while in prayer for the people of the Congo, I was interceding for them for unity and peace, which only God can give. I also prayed for the healing of the brokenhearted and the brokenness of the people. The Lord showed me 10 lame and that I was to humbly wash their feet as Jesus washed the disciples' feet. Carefully, and slowly going one by one explaining Jesus and his origins and purpose, praying and taking the good confession of the people. As this was done, I saw the cripples being healed. The vision became clearer. The people were sitting on chairs, milk cartons or on logs and were almost clear enough to see faces. It is going to happen. He will show me when and what to say for the healing of the people. More details Lord, more details – Amen.

In a vision I saw leprosy – a severe skin disease. Then I taught on instant healing – and the healing that occurred as the lepers that Jesus healed received as they were going. I suppose if the person had the faith to interrupt the meeting it would be instant, and otherwise it would be as they were going. Also I taught on the "other nine" lepers.

-- The seed pod became a mighty walnut tree.-- I was reminded of the walnut tree I planted as a boy-- and saw other trees in a drought, but the walnut tree prospered.

7-09-08 I had a dream about a machine out in the parking lot of a business. It was fairly large, about 3 feet by 3 feet by 10 inches thick. It was up on a pedestal and it looked like a vending machine. It had been there awhile because it was dirty and faded by the sun. It had a jump rope attached to the front for children to play with. Upon closer examination it had a slot for quarters and a sign that said " Ask any question" I got the impression or perhaps it said "nothing too hard or too easy". I had a dime and I put it into the coin slot, then the machine had text on the computer screen that said " ask your question" I didn't have a question because I was just playing with the machine to see what it did. I pressed the coin return button, and out came my dime. I pressed the coin return button again, and I got another dime and a nickel. I pressed it again and quarters started pouring out until it got ridiculous. The machine spit out a real stack of quarters, like a wheelbarrow full. I had nothing to put them in, and I couldn't believe the pile of money. I tried to borrow a bag, but then I woke up.

7-11-08 I saw another vision when I was at the Lakeland revival. I saw a small curved bridge that went across a small brook in the middle of a field or pasture that was as green as a golf course. The bridge was actually arched across the brook. I approached the bridge on an enduro type motorcycle The shape of the bridge changed and the arch became a ramp and when I hit the ramp I got air-born and did a flip in the air and went down the other side. I also need to write down the vision of David and the five stones.

David and the small stones. I remember this vision like it was yesterday. I was in prayer at the Ignited Church in Lakeland Florida. It was in the middle of the worship service. I received a mental picture. The picture looked like a stone, a small oval dark blue stone, with a bump that stuck up on one end. Then I was watching David picking up stones out of the brook. The Lord was telling David which stones to pick up. "This stone David, no, that stone David." Just Like that. David was carefully picking up the stones one by one. The blue stone was the one David was to use first. He placed it in the sling, and spun the sling around his head. At just the right second, he released the stone and it sped towards Goliath. The problem was that from Goliaths perspective the stone appeared like it was going to miss him. The path the stone was taking was going to bring the stone near to Goliath, but it was going to miss him. When the stone looked like it was going to miss, Goliath started to smile and chuckle to himself. Suddenly, the stone hooked like a bowling ball can when thrown by the hands of a professional. The stone hooked and hit Goliath right between the eyes. Goliath was the most surprised person on the battle field that day.

When I finally left for Africa, I went to London first, and spent a few days there. Why not, it was pretty much on the way. Besides, I had not gotten the visa that I needed in order to enter the Congo yet. I was a stickler about this. Edo assured me that I could just get the visa in Congo. The whole thing was just about the money. I know what a pain the US government is about visas. If you are from a poorer country, a visa could take months or years to get. I was concerned that I would get to Congo, and then it would become a giant nightmare getting the visa. I had already bought the $2,000 ticket, so I should have just listened. In my western head, well trained in western ways, I just couldn't handle it. Edo was super busy dealing with all of the stuff we needed to organize for the revival. I essentially made her take a half day off and go down to the Congolese embassy to get the required visa because I was so concerned about it. Edo was a real good sport about these little idiosyncrasies. I am sure that in her mind, she was thinking "Why doesn't he just listen to me" If she was thinking that, she didn't say anything, and it didn't show. She was very understanding about going along with the way that I thought it should be done. It is cultural. Until you have had the experience it would be very difficult to grasp how things were actually done in Congo. Edo must have understood all of this.

When we got to the Congolese embassy, there was another man there in front of us that was having a fit because a friend of his was in the Congo and they were saying in the Congo that his friends' visa was fake, so he couldn't enter the country. Additionally the man was being threatened with deportation. It was a paperwork and money problem. The guy probably needed to bribe the immigration official, and he wouldn't do it. I have heard that they will say that there is some important paperwork missing, and hand you back your passport. You then have to slip a little cash into your passport, then everything is ok. I didn't have that experience. The embassy personnel did a nice job and I was on my way. I even got a letter to go with my visa explaining that it was genuine.

London is real nice, and is just full of history. I enjoyed seeing everything, and enjoyed spending time with Edo's family there. I attended the Bible study that she held in her house, and met all of the students that attended. The students were very excited about what Jesus was doing, and were very willing to go evangelize at almost any time.

After a few days in London, I prepared to go to Africa.

7-21-08 I arrived in Africa Yesterday. Landed in Nairobi, Kenya from London. The flight was uneventful, except that the seat I had was the only seat on the plane that was supposed to recline, yet it was broken and would not recline. As a result, sleep was very difficult. Since it was a night flight, I was very tired when I arrived in Nairobi. The first impression that I got of the Nairobi airport was that I had never seen a 747 land on a gravel runway before. Of course the landing strip was concrete, but the airport lacked the fanciness of the western world. I managed to sleep all the way to Kinshasa (The capital of the D. R. of the Congo) except that I awoke briefly to eat breakfast.

The Kinshasa airport was an absolute zoo. dirty looking, no amenities or infrastructure to speak of. Security men were everywhere, endless lines. Being admitted into the country was easy enough. At this point it is more difficult to find English speaking people, as French is preferred. After finally getting through immigration I was still by myself. I was approached by a man named Jojo or Nono or something like that, who said he was with Edo my co-worker in the vineyard. I spoke to Edo by phone, and she confirmed that she sent him. Jojo/Nono then took my passport and baggage claim ticket and disappeared. I was regretting that I let go of my passport so easily after I did it. It didn't take long for me to start wondering if I would see it or my luggage again.

> *The airport was simply bedlam. It reminded me of when I visited a friend of mine at a rehab for people with brain injuries in Sunrise, Fl. In the rehab, there were insane people wondering aimlessly, screaming for no reason, milling about and jabbering to themselves. This was the same, except there were policemen in the place, and everyone else seemed intent on keeping you off balance. It is somewhat like what they do at the carnival when they are about to take your money away. Everything was a formality, and to my foreign eyes everything seemed designed to inconvenience the traveler as much as possible. It was like they were intentionally spinning you mentally because it was to their advantage to do so. We in the west are used to regular baggage claim, and everything is computerized. In the Congo, nothing is computerized, and the baggage is shuttled from the plane a truckload at a time in an old pickup truck. The process took hours. We were in some sort of a lounge, waiting. The "VIP" lounge was nicer than the airport, but dated and worn, I was left there for some time by myself (at least there were no other English speaking people there). Eventually we got most of our bags.*

Long story short- the box containing the audio snake, the wireless microphones, and the drive rack was missing. After waiting and standing in line an hour or so, we put in a claim. It is my prayer that the boxes show up. It is possible that they will because they told us the cargo hold was full and all the bags wouldn't fit on the plane I came in on.

> *When Edo came to Kinshasa she left a few days before I did. We went to Heathrow together so I could help with the bags and give her a proper send off. We were running a little late and we arrived in Heathrow terminal 5 a little late. The Heathrow airport had just built a new terminal, and it was laid out in a confusing way. It was so new that the employees had not gotten used to it yet either. Their instructions about how to check in were either wrong or misleading, and the signs were unclear as well.*

When Edo finally went to get onto the plane, we were at the gate with minutes to spare. Her carry on bag was a nice one with wheels on it. The gatekeeper at British Airways spotted the bag, and asked her to put it in the gauge that determined the maximum bag size, and it didn't quite fit.

Their website states "one standard-sized bag - maximum size of the bag must not exceed 56x45x25cm (22x17.5x9.85in) (including wheels, pockets and handles)" The bag was within these tolerances, but the gauge that they used had rounded corners instead of square corners and that was the difference on whether or not the bag would fit. It was very close. The bottom line was that they were being difficult, using their only power to complicate life. She ended up missing the flight. Her other bag was already checked on the plane. It was a blue cooler with wheels on it so it could be pulled through the airport. We had placed microphones, microphone cables and some clothes in it. They pulled the cooler off of the plane, and she asked them to hold it until the next day. Well, they did hold it, but it never made the next flight. She found out in Kinshasa, but they had poor communication between Kinshasa and London and they never did find the bag. Part of the problem was that she flew British Airways to Brussels, and then Brussels airlines to the Congo.

Since we had already had a rough experience with one bag, we didn't relish the idea of losing the other one. The next day we had to drive through Kinshasa traffic and back out to the airport to meet the Kenya airlines flight at the appointed time. Since I was the one on the flight, they wouldn't allow Edo to come with me into the baggage claim area. This made everything more difficult because of the language barrier. The official language was French, but everyone mostly spoke in local dialects. I waited for the men to finish unloading the plane, after standing there for quite awhile I realized that it wasn't a Kenya Airlines plane. I finally found someone who spoke English, and he directed me to another building that had the Kenya Airlines office in it. After a little more difficulty, the bag was located.

When you are not in the actual terminal or baggage claim area, you are usually surrounded by and pestered by young men that want to carry your bags for you so they can collect a tip. I found this highly annoying because they are very quick to distract you. They can work in teams: one person distracts you while the other one grabs something of value if they can. It is very difficult and stressful to watch everything all of the time. That is not to say that the people are thieves, actually my experience is *the reverse, the people were mostly very kind and considerate, wonderful hosts and a pleasure to work with. That being said, I must also say that Edo had her cell phone and a little cash stolen out of the pocket of her purse.*

Once we had located the bag, I carried it out of the office, and immediately there was a young man there who had staked his claim to the prized tip. At Edo's direction I gave the bag to the man to carry. There was another man there who felt that he was the one who should be carrying the bag. Well, they started to try to wrestle the bag out of each others hands, and basically we were watching a fight. One of them was the winner, and he carried the bag, but we ended up tipping both of them. I stick out like a sore thumb, as a white man, so since I am obviously not local, they were probably imagining an enormous tip. I am sure that is how it happens sometimes. The normal tip for the locals is fifty cents or a dollar. In most developed nations it would not be unusual to tip a porter between $5 and $20. I am sure that people have come to the Congo and immediately tipped that amount of money so you can see why I was a super target. Once we made it to the airport parking lot we were immediately surrounded by children selling things plus others that were just begging. There was one small boy there that was probably five. The rest of the boys were between eight and twelve. I gave the small boy a few francs with instructions to the others that it was for him only. They wanted to take it from him, but they ended up behaving themselves until he could get away from them.

On into Kinshasa, my first impression was that it was like any other developing nation, dirty, with people everywhere doing what they want – selling things roadside and generally milling about. We traveled down a paved road for a bit and them turned off the pavement into a neighborhood that looked pretty rough. I met some of Edo's family. They were nice, and the house was beautiful inside. I was very tired, and I could hardly keep my eyes open. For lunch we had meat, fufu and caterpillars or bugs of some kind. Fufu is either corn meal or ground cassava (yucca) made into a mashed potato consistency. It doesn't have much flavor, but it is a local favorite. The bugs were not bad. We went on another road trip in the dark to another home past a stadium. (The Vodacom soccer stadium. It seats 200,000) I saw two or three revivals along the way. We went into a modest home with modest furnishings- again the people were very nice. The power kept going on and off. I slept like a rock and awoke refreshed.

7/22/08 Yesterday was interesting. My lost bag was recovered at the Airport. After a long and difficult search I found an English speaking man who was working in airport security. He indicated we should go to the baggage claim belt and wait for our bag. After 30 minutes or so I realized that the baggage being unloaded was from South Africa Airways, so we again inquired and found that Kenya Airways had an office upstairs. We went and recovered the box with the snake and microphones. Two of the porters got into a shoving match over whose job it was to carry the box. Edo's phone was stolen at some point along with $20.00 US. I had asked the Lord previously where the baggage was, and He showed me that my box was at the airport, and Edo's was still in London at the place where they were holding it for her.

While in prayer for Edo earlier that morning, I saw a large black claw like a cats claw. The claw was very sharp, and then I saw a lion. I realized or felt that she was the lion claw in the paw of the lion of the tribe of Judah. I also had a dream last night about a church that I used to attend in Englewood, Florida. They were changing the seating to face another way and there was also was a long and narrow staircase that lead into the basement. Interesting, because they don't have a basement. *I feel that the church must be changing direction, and that direction doesn't lead in a good way.*

Today I met Marcelle, a Congolese man that speaks English, along with his friend Levy. They were both believers. *They had heard that an English speaking man was in town, and they had come over to Edo's sisters house because they wanted to practice speaking English. They also invited me to speak at their English speaking club. I never made it to the club because the scheduling never worked out right.*

7/23/08 Last night, I spent the night at Edo's sisters house. The house is located in the Binza Ozona area of Kinshasha. Her sisters name is Marijose Mukeza, she was real nice. It was a little difficult to communicate because of the language barrier. Today Edo picked me up at her sister's house where I had been staying around 10 am. It was a fairly busy day because she had a few things she needed to pick up and we needed supplies for the lights for the revival. We also needed speaker cords and connectors. There were a few problems. First of all, being in the streets of the Congo is an experience, the streets are noisy with cars and people in the marketplace. In addition, the streets are very dirty with smoke from burning garbage, dust from the cars, and auto diesel fumes. Trash is everywhere. Most of the side streets are dirt with open sewers on both sides. Thank God the sewers don't smell too much, but by the look of them they should smell quite bad. The market we went to was full of commotion, but the biggest problem was that once you drove into the alley, you could not turn around or go another way. You were trapped. There was no other way out You had to back out, a slow process at best. If there was any trouble it would have been a real problem. Fortunately, in the area we were in it wasn't one of the trouble hot spots. The people were very civilized. I still kept my eyes open and kept watch, because there are some in every crowd. Desperation can cause stupid things to happen.

Getting what we needed was a challenge because my French is very limited, and they don't understand English. We were purchasing things that were slightly technical in nature, and Edo was unfamiliar with the technical terms in English. We finally got everything worked out, and it was OK, but it must have taken 3 frustrating hours to get everything. Not bad, but I could have done it in 30 minutes in any decent hardware store in the US. Time just doesn't matter in many places in the world like it does in the US.

Apparently the local custom is to try and help a stranger, and then expect some type of a reward, so all of the locals were trying to be very helpful, but they were actually making it harder. By that I mean they would try to track things down that you wanted or needed, but invariably it was the wrong item because of the language and technical barrier. Once we procured the speaker cables and connectors, extension cords and lights we were on our way.

> *Getting the lights was interesting. All of the voltage in the Congo is 220 volts, like Europe. They sold us a case of halogen bulbs, but they didn't have any fixtures, so they stripped some wire bare, wrapped and stapled it to some wood and voila, light fixtures. Anyone who would have touched the bare wire could have been electrocuted. That is just how they did things. As long as it worked, it was acceptable. For example, at one of the churches they were using a pair of extremely thin telephone wires as an extension cord for the lights. The telephone wire is barely thicker than a hair, and they were running 220 volts through it. I am surprised it even worked. The things we take for granted.*

> *The Congo is rich in copper. I heard that they dig up large chunks in the dirt the size of a baseball, or better, then they pick it out by hand. All of the high voltage wiring is underground It is large diameter copper as thick as a mans thumb. People dig it up and steal it, or it gets nicked and corrodes. They are constantly repairing it. The guy that repairs it might make a collection through the neighborhood to get enough money together to do the repairs. He doesn't actually work for the power company or anything like that. They are just the local guys that live in the neighborhood and do the power repairs. It would be as if you didn't have any power, and the power company took too long to fix the problem, so you just did it yourself. Since the local repair guy is repairing it, he gets paid. He has no incentive to repair it completely with the correct tools and supplies, because then he would be out of work. What they do is patch it up with splices and electrical tape. Then it gets wet, and corrodes or the load gets too great and it burns in two, or it shorts out, then they fix it again. To compound the problem, there are many, many places where the bare wiring is exposed, many times without proper insulation. You have to watch your step because stepping on bare high voltage lines on the ground can be fatal. The problem is worse during the rainy season because the wire can be lying on the bottom of a puddle, and all the ground around it can be charged with high voltage. I was told that many people die of electrocution in the rainy months.*

Edo had sent her sister Marijose to the small Ndolo airport in Kinshasa, not the *N'djili* International airport, to secure tickets to Kikwit. While we were on the way to the airport, she called to inform Edo that the flight was sold out. When we arrived at the airport, a man walked up to us and spoke to Edo and before we knew it, we had tickets to Kikwit. There is some sort of a system perhaps involving bribery or favoritism. Perhaps they sell tickets at the counter for one price, and he has a deal worked out where he buys them and resells them at a higher price. Or perhaps the counter can only sell so many tickets at the low price, and then after that they have to see this man. I don't know, it was just strange. When you think about it, the airline ticket buying process is very strange in this country also. The computers are forever forecasting demand, and changing prices. Who are we to criticize the system they have worked out, just because it is not how we do it.

> *The airport landing strip was paved, but the parking lot wasn't. There was a terminal of sorts. It amounted to a bunch of counters that were outside, but under roof, an indoor waiting area, a guard shack and a couple of hangars. It was a step or two above a dirt landing strip, all in all functional but primitive. There was a big open market at one end of the runway. In January of 1996 a 35 year old Russian built turboprop was taking off over 600 lbs overweight. It had overshot the end of the runway and had run into the market and killed 297 people. Those things happened in Africa, and before you knew it the market would be repaired, and people would be right back there in the market again, oblivious to the dangers.*

Once the tickets were secured, we went to Edo's other sisters' house and relaxed. Her name was Genevieve Mukeza. Her house is located in Lemba. Lemba had a 100 foot tall needle shaped tower in the middle of it. The tower was some kind of a decorative government project. They were preparing live eels for dinner, which was OK with me because I like eel. We didn't stay for dinner so we went to Edo's other sister's house that was further from downtown, where I was staying. We had dinner. I packed for the trip because we were leaving the next day, then went to sleep.

> *Remember the open sewers? Well if you think that they go to a sewer treatment plant, and then the sewage is treated and disposed of properly, think again. The open sewers are more like a mini canal system that eventually dumps into the Congo river. "Dumps" is the correct word, like taking a dump in the river. OK so the river*

is polluted, and all the streams run a nice grey color, like greywater or effluent. In the Congo, people sell fish on the side of the road. Fresh fish are just hanging there from a rope along the road. A country that essentially doesn't have refrigeration. Where do you think the fresh fish and the live eels come from? The river. At least they are well cooked, they got that down. Everything is well cooked. I even saw them fishing in the greywater streams. Streams almost completely covered with plastic bottles and floating trash, but that didn't stop the fishermen. Like they say "you gotta eat."

7-24-08 I woke up at 3am and up again at 5am. *It was one of those nights, couldn't sleep, up late packing, restless from the excitement about the events ahead.* It was 5am and I was running late. Edo wasn't staying at the same house. She had just arrived. We packed our things into the vehicle and waited for the driver to arrive and take us to the airport. It seemed like an eternity because I was ready to go. I was all excited about the trip and we were already running behind. The flight was at 6am, it was already after 5am and it takes at least 30 minutes to get to the airport. I was calculating the length of the trip to the airport, and doing the math in my head. It didn't look like we were going to make it. Edo told me that the flight probably wouldn't leave until 12:30pm, but I didn't believe her. In my western ways and western mind, we were going to miss the flight if we didn't hurry up. *She was very understanding about my way of thinking, and patient. She went along with what I felt was necessary so that I wouldn't feel uneasy. She really could have told me that the flight was at 12:30 and it would not have been possible for me to know any different. Then she would not have had to put up with my nervousness about being late. That would have been a lie, and it was not in her character to do things like that. Even the little "white" lies are still lies.* Once we got underway, the driver remembered that we needed some empty gas cans because he was driving to Kikwit in the Nissan with the land rover following. The gas cans were in the garage, so it was only a short delay, but it ended up making me more nervous. *The Land Rover really did have to follow us on the paved road. It was a diesel, and only capable of about 45mph. Once we hit the trails it really shined, it only took a few minutes, and then it was so far ahead of us we could no longer see it.*

We arrived at the airport a little after 6am. Inside I was a wreck because we were so late, outside I was trying hard not to show it. We unpacked and checked in, and sat down. I was apparently going to have plenty of time. The airport was like the market, with vendors wondering up to us to show us CD's, bread, candy, gum, cigarettes you name it. It is the same stuff that is everywhere. Street hustlers. They wanted to carry the bags as usual, getting uncomfortably close. I know about pickpockets in the U.S., and if they do it in the U.S., they do it everywhere. Because they aggravated me, I didn't let them get close to the bags, and just carried them myself. I started wondering around, got bored and decided to take a picture of the front of the airport. Somebody spotted me taking a picture, so I was called over to where the guards were (with their Russian assault rifles) and reprimanded for taking a picture. Fortunately, I didn't speak much French (although I could basically understand it) so they had to call the boss, who called his boss, who spoke English. Meantime they went and got Edo. The argument started in English, and then quickly went to Lingala. Edo doesn't like the bribery system, and doesn't mind telling them so. The whole thing was about the fact that they had caught me in an infraction, and now they had the right to extricate money. Since I was from the west, I had dollars, and now they were going to get some. I showed them that I could delete the picture, then I deleted it. (I recently found out that it is possible to recover deleted photo's so that will be a new project for me) They said that it was a $10.00 fine which I gladly borrowed the money from Edo, and paid. What they didn't know was that I had taken a photo of the airport the day previous, which I still have :). I then went to the waiting room and kept my head low like a puppy that had just gotten into trouble; doing my best not to aggravate Edo further.

We found out that our flight would leave around 9 am, so about that time we headed towards the plane. As we walked towards our plane, interestingly enough, I spotted three complete Douglas DC3's along with some very old Cessna's that had been sitting in one place so long that they were covered in mildew and looked to be out of service. There were a few other old planes there as well. Our plane was a 16 passenger turboprop that looked pretty new from a distance. As we approached I realized that it was probably 20 to 30 years old. I inspected it as we approached, and it looked ok. There was one spot where it looked like a prop blade had flown off and hit the fuselage or cabin area of the plane. They had repaired it with a piece of aluminum riveted over the hole, so it was good by African standards. When I went to get on board, the steps broke under my weight (6' 02", 200+/- lbs). They tried to put them back, but they broke again, right where the steps attach to the threshold of the door. I climbed in over the steps and got into the plane. There were two seats open, but someone had already placed their luggage under the seat in front of us, where our carry on luggage would have gone. My 6'02" frame ended up crammed into the window seat with a bag on my lap, and Edo's laptop on the floor. I could sit, but I couldn't really move. It was ok until the flight was half over, then the pain in my foot got to where I needed to move the foot. So I wiggled around and the pain went away. The flight had coffee and rolls available, and it was pretty good.

> *They fired up the engines and we sat on the runway waiting for the engines to warm up, and for everyone to be ready. I was just sitting there looking out the window, then I noticed a stream of fluid pouring out of the engine on my side of the plane. It was a pretty good stream, about like a faucet that is running at a pace better than just a drip. I pointed it out to Edo, and then to the flight attendant. The flight attendant said "It always does that, it will quit when we take off". Perfect. I am not convinced it quits, I think the wind rushing over the engine turns the small stream into droplets we cannot see. Well, I said a prayer, and then took comfort in the fact that the Lord is in control, and He didn't bring us all the way there to do His work, just to let us perish in a plane crash. I actually inquired about it, and had peace, so I knew it would be fine.*

After we took off, it was smoky outside but I could see some of the terrain, it looked rough, but the vegetation was not as thick as Florida, or the jungles of Brazil. The terrain reminded me of the jungles of Costa Rica on the dry Pacific side, beautiful and difficult to travel through, but it could be done.

The arrival in Kikwit was very interesting. Edo lead the way, walking past the president and coordinator of the "Equipping the Heroes" ministry and up to the officials that wanted to see our documents. I had forgotten my Yellow Fever certificate, and had been fined $10.00 for the error at the N'dolo airport in Kinshasa. I was bracing for another fine. About this time, the president recognized Edo, and realized where she was. We were then surrounded by 20 or so pastors that were wishing us well. The VIP treatment started. There were at least 75 singers there that started praising the Lord. Then all of the singers had to kiss us on both cheeks. Next, about 10 little girls about 12 yrs old started to dance for us. They danced a slow dance up to us, and then presented us with flowers. The girls were adorable, all dressed up, and doing this slow rhythmic dance/march in our direction. Next, we were greeted by a line of at least 75 well wishers. While they were greeting us, I felt the Holy Ghost all around us. I blessed them all as we were greeted in English. Once the formalities were over we went to sit in the lounge to wait on paperwork while the greeters carried off our bags. When people from the church surrounded us, I didn't mind because I knew their intentions were good. We sat in the lounge for an hour, then we were allowed to leave. I later learned that the local officials allowed us to return later to fill out the necessary paperwork. Congo is not like the US. Once you are in the US, you are free to go anywhere on any road in the entire country. In the Congo, each region is like a state, and you have to register and pay a fee if you arrive and you intend to stay for more that just a day or so.

We got into one of the cars, and headed to town. We were basically in a parade of 10 or so cars. Edo and I were in a car towards the front of the convoy, and she stood up on the seat and popped up through the sunroof of the car she was in so she could wave at the crowds.(I was in the back seat) The other cars were honking their horns and shouting into bullhorns announcing the revival. We proceeded on the drive into town for the next 30 to 40 minutes. Both sides of the road were lined with well wishers until we arrived at the church. There were shouts of joy, and a man was saying something I did not understand. Horns were honking furiously as people waved, and wanted to shake hands with Edo. It was quite an honor. They said later that they were greeting us, but actually they were greeting the Lord. I felt that the Lord wants to bless these people greatly, and that the town will be blessed for generations as a result of all of this. Praise God.

We went to the church, and there was a brief welcoming ceremony, then we went to the hotel. The hotel was a spartan building that apparently used to be an old convent, or something like that. Fairly clean and comfortable, but sparse. It reminded me of a $15.00 per night hotel in Costa Rica, very basic, but safe and dry. The story was the same as far as the power was concerned. On and off all the time. I asked one of the translators if he could get a schedule for me of when the power was going to be turned on or off. It puzzled him for a few minutes, so he asked Edo about it, and then I told her I was joking with him. They all got the joke and laughed. Usually jokes don't translate well. I was able to fire off a few emails from the hotel because they had an internet cafe there. At 5pm this evening, there will be a meeting where the particulars will be discussed about the start of the meeting tomorrow. I expect the Lord will do some marvelous things. I am very excited, and cannot wait. Bless the Lord. Amen.

I met with the pastors. The whole meeting was in either French or Lingala, so I didn't catch much. Edo brought a praise team from Kinshasa to Kikwit. They were traveling by SUV, but their vehicle had broken down on the side of the road outside of Kinshasa. Edo was told this by a prophet 2 days ago. I am sure he was a prophet, and I don't want to take away from the prophecy, but after traveling on these roads and seeing the vehicle maintenance programs, breaking down on the roads was a more likely event than not. As of 7:30 am on 7-25-08 the worship team is either still broken down, or they are limping this way. Essentially, all of the pastors agreed it was going to be a big blessing for the city. We went to the radio station, which is one of 3 in the area. The station is 100% Christian owned and operated. It has no denominational affiliations. It reaches a

200km diameter, out to a potential audience of 6 million people according to the radio station staff. Mostly they wanted to interview Edo, but they wanted to hear what the Lord had me doing there as well.

> *The radio station was interesting because all of the equipment was extremely old and broken down. The men managed to keep it running most of the time even though it was ancient. I feel that there is a tremendous opportunity in the Congo for upgrading the existing radio stations, getting licenses for new stations, and then preaching the Gospel. The government is very supportive of all this, but it still takes tremendous financial resources.*

7-26-08 We still have no power, and now there is no water. The hotel had a 750 gallon or so reserve tank above the third floor. We were staying on the third floor, but it wasn't high enough above the third floor that you could draw out 100% of the water. I think that was so they could collect the water off of the roof when it rained. There was water in the tub in the only bathroom on the floor, and I finally figured out that it was the emergency reservoir. I was able to clean up using a bucket full of water. The only time I ever took a bath out of a bucket before I went to the Congo was once after hurricane Charlie passed 15 miles south of my house. Now I am clean. In the hotel, all meals were included, breakfast was bread and coffee, and the refrigerator was a very disgusting moldy science project at best. We didn't eat much food from there, as it was mostly rotten. The driver was supposed to pick us up at 8am to take us to the conference. They picked us up a little while after 8 am. Time runs slower in Africa, and schedules are more like a suggestion. When in Rome, eh? The morning session was in the church we first went to. The church was a fairly large 50' x 75' building with concrete walls, a tin roof and a dirt floor. Primitive by American standards, pretty nice for Congo. They still managed to get almost 500 people in there. The morning session was geared towards preparing the church for the afternoon session. Again it was 99% in French and Lingala, so I didn't really follow it. The music was nice, and the people seemed to enjoy it.

I saw another white person in the church. How interesting. It was a woman that looked to be in her late 20's or early 30's. I thought she must be a missionary from the US, or Europe. I later realized that she was an albino. It is a rare condition, however, I actually saw about as many albinos in Congo as I did white people.

When I was in Florida I really had a strong desire to buy sunblock lotion. We get a strong tropical sun in Florida, and sunblock is a good idea if you are going to be outside all day. If you are not used to the sun, it will burn you very severely if you are not wearing sunblock. I am used to the sun, so it doesn't cause me to blister. I realized that we were going to be very near the equator, and I knew that we could be outside for the revival, so this was something that I felt very strongly that I really needed. I even had to make a special trip to the store to get some. The funny thing is that I was running late so I decided that it would be easier to buy the sunblock in London. I then realized that they don't get a strong tropical sun, so that wouldn't work. I then thought that I would buy some in Congo. That was funny, because they probably don't have any in the entire country since they are naturally equipped for the hot sun.

A day or two after I first saw this albino girl, I saw her again. She had walked all the way to our hotel so that she could speak with Edo. I then realized that it was the Lord who had been giving me a strong sense of urgency about the sunblock, and that I had not brought the sunblock for myself, rather it was for the albino girl, so I then told her the story, and gave her the sunblock lotion.

After returning to our rooms we waited to be taken to the afternoon meeting. Edo and I spent most of the time preparing ourselves for the work of the Lord by studying the Bible and resting in God's presence. The afternoon session was in a large field on the outside of town with a small handmade stage. The speakers had blown woofers, so the sound had all of the distortion and buzz that is associated with overdriven speakers with damaged cones. The worship team finally made it, so all is well. There were at least 3 to 4,000 with possibly as many as 6000 people in attendance. People always bring their situations with them to a meeting like this, so sometimes it is like the worship is off if you know what I mean. It is like the people are distracted and not into it because of their issues. You know, when the crowd is more like an audience than active participants.

Edo's words and testimony were amazing, the people really related to what she was saying, and as a result over 6-700 people came and gave their lives to Christ. That night, I was praying and soaking in the Lord. I saw that we could invite the infirm up to the front and have them sit there, and then pray for them later. The point of it was so that they could be closer to the front so they could be up under the anointing and presence of the Lord. I saw a quick vision of an old handmade iron chain, and one of the links just broke.

7-27-08 I had a dream last night. The dream was like a video game. Edo and I were trapped in a large room, perhaps 35' x 35'. There was a large black bird in there with a strong black beak similar to a toucan, only smaller. The bird was perhaps 15' tall and was chasing us around the room. I had a strategy. I sent Edo back into the room because we had temporarily escaped out of a small door. The bird could not catch her, so she was safe doing this. When the bird noticed her, it gave chase and she went out the door. The bird was large enough that only its head could fit out of the door. When it stuck its head through the door, I was standing just outside the door, and I chopped off its head. End of bird, end of story. *I believe the point of the dream was that we get strategies from the Lord, and we have to pay attention, additionally we have to work together, and it is not without perceived risks.*

Today in the morning session, a Muslim man came and testified that he was into witchcraft and that he didn't know about the conference, but he had dreamed about it. He gave his life to Christ. While praying for him, I saw a wing of an airplane, I believe that the Lord is sending him to the nations, so I released that word to him. The meeting was good, about prospering, breaking curses and unity. During the meeting, I was indoors, but I kept feeling raindrops. It is a really strange sensation, you feel the rain like it is really raining, but it is not. The drops are prophetic. However, it did rain that night, and since it had been so dry, that was prophetic too. An abundance of rain.

7-27-08pm The afternoon conference, day two. I felt that I was supposed to warm up the crowd a bit, share my vision of the diamonds, call people up front that needed healing, and then introduce Edo. It was interesting. I don't think the people truly understood that they were to be involved, and were to press into the Lords presence. It seemed that they were difficult to get involved. We worshiped a little, and I encouraged them to engage, focus and worship, but I was feeling a disconnect. I pressed through during a song, and then switched to the vision of the diamonds, which they liked. The platform was exactly like the vision, so it was cool. After that I called for the sick and infirm to come up front and sit in the anointing. They didn't really understand what I was trying to get them to do. It could have been a translation problem. It was all a little confusing. I introduced Edo and had her explain it to them, then went to sit down. As I sat down I felt like I had said "Our God is great and He can do miracles, come up here and get your miracle now. Ok Edo, here is the microphone, show them how it is done." It was a little awkward to say the least. Edo was a real trooper, to walk into that mess and fix it. She handled it very well. She gave her message, it was a very good message and the people received it well. After the message we began to pray for the sick. It started a little slow, but as we progressed down the line there was a boy with a withered hand. I felt that it was going to be healed. There was some improvement, but it was not completely healed at that time. Jesus healed some right away, and others gradually or as they went in faith. There was a boy that looked to be about 12 who was stone deaf, and as a result, he couldn't speak. Edo told me later that he could now hear, Praise God. It was like that. People had problems and it was difficult for me to know what the problem was. They would get healed and due to the language barrier it could be two days before I heard about it. That was just the way it was. There was a woman there who looked so skinny and sick, like she had AIDS, and her baby was sick too. We prayed for both of them. One woman gave me her dying baby to hold, I held it and prayed, then I felt the presence whoosh through me, so I believe that child was healed as well.

There was an elderly sickly looking woman that looked like she had AIDS that was sitting on the ground. Her legs were so thin they looked like pencils. We prayed for her, and pressed in. She began to stretch out and walk. A definite healing. The crowd went wild and then they all started to come forward. I was praying for many children. I was in such a deep level of prayer during this time. Unfortunately, the crowd was getting difficult, so we had to stop. We stopped by the church near the revival where the intercessors were praying, but we didn't go in, then we went to the radio station. Edo and I did a nice 10 minute interview with John Minanga in English that was to be broadcast on local radio 102.5. the interview went well. We just told them who we were and why we were there. After the meeting we went to meet with the worship team. It was very interesting and a couple of them spoke a little English. As soon as I got to my room, opened the door and just as I turned on the light, the power went off in the whole city for the night.

7/28/08 Today was amazing. I went to a small church of 300 or so that was just past the location of the revival in Kikwit. The Living Stone Church. I spoke on Jonah and the great commission. The church said they liked the message. I prayed for those who felt they were like Jonah, as well as for those who gave their lives to Christ at the revival. John Minanga translated for me, he was concerned that he could not understand my accent. It was pretty funny to me because I don't have a heavy accent, but it is definitely not British. I found out today that the sickly woman with the legs like pencils was paralyzed. She had to be carried to the revival. I heard that she walked back home healed. *We had the entire revival videotaped, but most of the video didn't turn out due to a technical glitch. There is video of this woman on Youtube as well as africarevival.com* That the deaf mute boy we prayed for heard. The formerly Muslim boy was also at church Sunday morning.

That evening, Edo spoke powerfully on her life and on the presence of God. The crowd had increased to perhaps 5-6,000 people. When the question was asked " Do you want the presence of God in your life, they came- slowly at first, then the rush began. Ultimately an area 90-100' in front of the stage and back on both sides about that far was full of people shoulder to shoulder, at least 8-900 people, possibly as many as 1000. they all gave their lives to Christ in prayer.

The local pastors all came and brought dirt from their area as a representation of the land. The land was all placed together, unified, and then anointed with oil. Then they all prayed. The people were all told to find one of the local churches after the the revival.

I felt the prophetic raindrops again. I told the people about the raindrops and that it meant that the drought was over – the Lord was blessing Kikwit. It was a total victory and the people really felt it. During the day we had moved into a new hotel, and it was the nicest one of the whole trip. It used to be a brothel, but now it is a hotel. After the meeting, we went to our new rooms and had a victory dinner, eggs, cassava, sardines and bread.

7/29/08 Monday. There was a Pastors meeting at 10:00 am. I found out about it just before we left, so I didn't get a chance to shower, shave or anything. I was wearing just jeans and a t-shirt. Edo did mention it a few days ago, but I had forgotten about it. The meeting was about finances and was all in French and Lingala. I couldn't follow it, so it was very boring to me, so I mostly engaged the Lord. After the meeting we walked through town and visited Edo's relatives. I always tell them hello, and then sit back while they chat. We went to a cousins' house, she was very sick. I had her accept Jesus and rededicate her life, and I prayed fervently for her. She felt the fire of God. I believe the Lord showed me that He was the water of life. I had them fetch me a glass of water, I prayed over it and told her to drink a little bit every day for three days.

I have never liked the death bed conversions. They are better than nothing, but they are so difficult emotionally. Sometimes people aren't in their right minds due to pain or the medications. Additionally, the Bible clearly teaches water baptism by immersion as an important part of the conversion process, and many times the people are too sick for this. (see the conversion of the Ethiopian Eunuch in Acts chapter 8 for example) I don't have to sort them out or judge them, but I can say this "remember the Lord your God in the days of your youth" because you can be well taught and effective in the kingdom. That way you won't miss out on all of the blessings He has for you.

This morning, which is Tuesday, I had a quick dream of Edo's dying cousin. The dream was at the dining room table. There were small pieces of very sharp glass on the table. They had been feeding it to her. I realized she was being poisoned. I knew she had stomach problems, and I believe the Lord revealed the source. *She was going to be moved to a pastors house, whose wife was a nurse, and then to Kinshasa. Logistically we did not have time to see to all of that, and about a month after we returned to civilization, we heard that she had died.*

After walking in town, and in the market we went back to the church. The young children are fascinated by seeing a white man so they all want to meet me and shake my hand. It is really fun for me too. They are not really sure what to think, they are a little afraid of me. Once, when several boys got close, I jumped a little and they were all startled. They got the joke, and then we all laughed and had fun. At the church we met with the intercessors, ushers and helpers. It was very nice, but a bit formal. Afterwards we took pictures. There was a girl there with spike hair, we had our picture taken by one of the men. I spotted a big all wheel drive transport truck. The truck had a monkey tied to it, so I took a picture of the truck and the monkey. The man who took my picture a few moments previous said that he would get me a monkey, but he wanted an English Bible. Perfect – a pet monkey of my very own. *True confession time... I took (stole?) a Gideons Bible from a hotel so that I would have an extra one in the Congo. It ended up to be a good thing that I did because Edo needed to keep borrowing it. I think hers had too small of type, or something. Anyway, I met a man that wanted the Bible. He offered to swap that Bible for a monkey. I wanted to do it because it would be fun to have a monkey for a minute or two. After I was done with the monkey I could just let the monkey go, or give it away. In the mean time one of the translators begged Edo for the Bible so much that he ended up with it. So I felt that the Bibles in hotel rooms are there to spread the word, and the hotel gets them for free, so if I took one did I steal it? See how the rationalization process works. It wasn't mine, and I took it. I repent Lord.*

7-30-08 I met with Edo, Guillermo, the formerly Muslim boy and Elias. We prayed together. The Lord gave me a detailed word for Guillermo in order to encourage him through the coming trials. The word was confirmed with a vision of an elderly mother or grandmother who walked with a cane, worked in a kitchen, wore a blue hat and dress, was heavy, and had a name with an "R" in it like Ruth. It was all correct except the "R" and Ruth part. Perhaps her life is like Ruth's, I don't know. It was cool, and I am sure he was encouraged.

Until 3 pm on the 30th Edo and I mostly hung out at the Hotel as person after person showed up to talk to her. She was very gracious and spoke to everyone. At 3pm the Pastors showed up and we went to the Pastors house that was the head of the association for lunch. The food was good, eel, fufu, pineapple, oranges, cassava, and sweet potatoes. All the children in the neighborhood showed up, between 30 and 50 children all outside looking in the windows and doors from a distance hoping to get a glimpse of the white man. They called me Mundaylay, a Lingala word for white man that literally means something like ghost man, walking dead man, or zombie or something like that. It is not particularly flattering, but they don't mean anything by it. The children were a little afraid of me, but they all wanted to shake my hand. I think it was for bragging rights to their friends " I saw a white man, and I even got to shake his hand." It was a circus, surrounded by excited children that all wanted to say hello.

The land rover that Edo bought in the UK showed up. It was totally sweet, older and a diesel. A completely classic land rover. We were on safari for sure now. After Lunch, we went to Edo's relatives by the church, and ate again, the same basic staples. God must have made eels to feed Africa, they are popular here. We also ate some mushroom stuff that wasn't bad. When we got home to the hotel, Blaise was there waiting. He is a man that I met earlier. I am not sure what he wants, just to speak English I suppose – but the real issue is probably funding for his ministry "In Gods Mighty Hand" I don't know, he seems very interested in talking to me at length. They show up, the people that want a piece of it. No doubt. It is up to the Lord, not me, thank God.

I wanted to go to the internet, but I procrastinated because I thought they might be closed. Additionally it may have been because it involved a ¾ mile walk down a totally unlit street full of potholes late at night. Once I finally decided to go, when I got to the store I found out that they closed in 10 minutes. I know that if I spoke French or Lingala I could have probably convinced them to stay open. Well, it will just have to wait until Wednesday – Gungu trip day.

7-31-08 Wednesday Up at 7 am or so. I got everything packed shortly thereafter and now we are waiting for the vehicles. Since I was all packed and ready, at 8am I went to the internet cafe to try and straighten out the mess with Denise, Olivia, Mom and the emails.

You see, the problem is with the internet in the Congo. It seems slower than dialup, and to make matters worse, you can be in the middle of writing an email and then the power goes out suddenly, and you lose your work. As a solution, I wanted to send emails to one person in the US who would then send it on to everyone on the list. That way I could keep people abreast of what was happening without the difficulty of doing everything from the Congo. Since I was in Sarasota, Florida when I left the U.S., I asked my friends Denise and Olivia to do it for me, because I knew they were on the computer most of the day. Unfortunately, it proved to be a poor choice only because I was adding to their already heavy workload. I then asked my retired mother to do it. I knew she would because her only son was half way around the world in a difficult place. Mom and Denise exchanged emails and got it all worked out.

I guess the situation with the emails will take care of its self. By 8:30 I was back from the internet and all of the luggage is getting packed on the Jeeps. The Nissan had a bad wheel cylinder on the right front, and the mechanic charged $110 to fix it, and only replaced a couple of seals. Its ok I guess, but the wear indicator is rubbing.

At least that is what I thought was going on. They said the problem was the disc so I thought the disc was the disc brakes, when in fact they were referring to the clutch disc. They call the clutch the disc. So I had them check the brake disc, and it was not functioning 100%, but that wasn't the biggest problem. The problem is that the sand is very deep on the road to Kikwit, and it destroyed a clutch on the way there. It was repaired, and we were on the way.

We gather together to ask the Lords blessing for the rest of the trip, then we are underway. After a short drive we stop to fuel up. There are very few proper gas stations in the Congo, most of them are in the capital. In Kikwit the fuel depot had a giant all wheel drive Mercedes truck in it that looked like it was full of 55 gallon drums filled with fuel. While some of the men were unloading the truck, there were other men changing one of the tires on the big fuel truck. We pulled into the entrance, blocking the exit of the big truck. Fortunately, the truck wasn't going anywhere soon because of the repairs being performed. The driveway was only a car width wide, blocked on one side by a building, and on the other side by a concrete wall. The Land Rover pulled in behind us, blocking our exit as well. Now we were trapped by the big fuel truck in front, the Land Rover behind us, a building and a concrete wall. There was just enough room on one side for a person to squeeze through, and on the other side there was just enough room so the workers could roll a 55 gallon drum through the sand up to the Nissan so it could refuel. They began pouring diesel fuel and gasoline out of 55 gallon drums rolled up next to the vehicles into buckets. The fuel was then siphoned into the vehicles. Fuel splashed on the ground, onto the drums, covered the siphon hoses, sloshed out of the buckets and ran down the sides of the vehicles. One spark and the vehicles would be on fire with no escape. Thank God the gasoline never ignited, the ensuing scene would have been horrific. Such is Africa, blindly forward, oblivious to the danger.

On the road to Gungu at last. We followed a wide slow river, and ended up crossing it twice. The first crossing was near town, there were the usual shanty shops all along the way down both sides of the road. Food is a problem because there aren't any restaurants and power is out most of the time, so refrigeration is not possible. This was an especially difficult issue for me because I was not acclimated to the local microbes, and I probably don't have to explain what they can do. The locals that were traveling with us just bought food from the roadside vendors, I didn't want to chance it. As we got out of town the traffic got lighter until there was practically none. There were occasional villages that had huts in them that were made out of bamboo covered with mud. The villages had goats running around, plenty of small children, and occasional booths by the road selling things. We stopped in one village, and all the locals ran up to the vehicle to sell bananas and peanuts. We all ate – I just ate the bananas because I knew they were ok.

Finally the Land rover caught up with us and we all took off. We drove until the pavement ended, we turned right down a jeep path full of real fine sand. The trail continued for several hours. By this time there was a thin film of fine sand everywhere. We couldn't keep the windows up because it was warm out, and we were the middle vehicle. I finally explained to our driver that if he allowed some space between ourselves and the vehicle ahead, we wouldn't have to eat as much dust. The trail did get occasional maintenance, I even saw the road grader they used to fix up the path. What they did was push the loose sand to the side of the road. This resulted in real high piles of sand down both sides of the road, and we were essentially driving down the middle of a long pit. The piles were usually only a couple of feet high, however, at times they were over six feet high, so we were actually traveling six feet below the natural grade.

A couple of times we crossed a small creek on a little bridge. There were always children swimming, some were naked, and they were mostly boys. Edo said I should take a picture. The problem is that the world is sick, and I didn't want anyone to see the pictures and think I was sick as well.

The terrain was arid and very dusty, but the mango trees seemed to survive, so it wasn't dry enough to kill them. The mango trees got huge, and a big mango tree can produce bushels and bushels of mangos. In Kinshasa, there were mango trees growing along the road, and here and there. Instead of leaving them alone and enjoying the fruit, poor people would get desperate for firewood, so they would cut a little bark off of the mango trees. This would continue over time until the mango trees were essentially girdled. They would then produce less and less fruit, grow weak and die. It is like a focus on short term results rather than long term rewards. There is so much land in Africa, that if it was properly utilized, it could grow an abundance of food.

In the valleys, where the creek was, everything was lush, tropical and green. As we traveled, finally we went down a large, steep hill. At the bottom was a ferry in a river that was 100 to 150' across. The river was the same one we saw earlier, slow and powerful, with light rapids at one end. The ferry carried up to 2 cars at a time, and was set up so the river could provide propulsion based on the angle of attack of the ferry in relation to the flow of the river. It took almost four hours to cross the river with all three vehicles. Once across, we were in Gungu in 5 or 10 minutes.

Once we arrived the hoopla started. Mama Edo was in town, and she had a mundaylay with her. This was a big deal for this sleepy little town. The children were so excited. There was over 100 of them running alongside of the vehicles for almost two miles. We were driving pretty slow, so it wasn't that difficult for them to keep up. They all wanted to shake my hand as they were running next to the car. I complied at first, then it began to get dangerous, so I had to stop. We stopped at the "Hotel", there was no electric, and no running water, my bed consisted of slats covered with a mattress. You could feel the slats as you lay on the bed. I'm tired, hungry, no food in sight, the mattress was very uncomfortable. Still I didn't complain.

7-??-08 Thursday OK, they finally showed up with the food. I suppose it is good in a way that they assigned someone to cook all the food – cassava, potatoes, something like spinach, and something like grits, called semolina. This morning we waited for a long time, then we finally got coffee, bread and avocados for breakfast. It was avocado sandwiches, in case you didn't figure it out. For some reason they included ketchup. I never had an avocado sandwich before, even though I love ketchup on almost everything, but it doesn't sound good on avocado sandwiches. The local coffee here is quite good, very low in acidity. *Thank God they even have coffee, it is one of the pleasures I would find hard to live without. I would place the coffee on par with a good Costa Rican blend. I should know because I owned a coffee shop at one point. The logistics of getting the coffee out of the local area where it is grown, and out to the market would be a complete nightmare. That is probably why it is not exported. They grind it to a very fine powder, and I place it in the cup with hot water and drink it cowboy style...grounds and all. Because it is ground so fine, the grounds sink to the bottom so it is not all that bad.*

The reason they had assigned a cook to cook all of the food was because of the fear of witchcraft. It is a well founded fear, because witchcraft does exist, and it is not just in the jungles of Africa, it is even in your hometown, you just don't always recognize it. The witches would poison us if they got the opportunity. Edo had some pants washed by the person who was selected by the local church leaders. Once the pants were washed, someone else was assigned to watch them until they dried – again due to the fear of witchcraft. We rebuke all witches and all witchcraft and all demonic assignments now in Jesus name and declare that all curses return to those who spoke them sevenfold.

The bread had sand in it, mostly due to the way the wheat is stored and how the flour is prepared and stored. Everything is done outdoors in the open. Some lady is outdoors now pounding something in a large wooden log or stump that has a top shaped like a bowl, with a pole about 3" in diameter.

I have been trapped in the hotel all day. My nickname for this hotel is the "Goat Hotel" because of all of the goats and chickens that are roaming everywhere. The owner is buried on the property about 50 feet from the western entrance to the hotel. There is no water or electricity. Apparently the town generator is off line because they decided to pour a pad for it to set on. It will be a few days before the concrete is ready. Sooner or later we will have to go to immigration. Pastor Al Davis is supposed to send some support from Consuming Fire Int'l Ministry, which is very nice. I cannot wait for the revival to begin tomorrow.

> There are a lot of people from Consuming Fire Int'l ministry that flow in the prophetic. About a year ago Pastor Al Davis, and Apostle Willie Peterson prophesied that everyone was supposed to get their passport because the Lord was going to open up some nations to the ministry. Well, its funny because no one did it, (I already had my passport) including those who prophesied. So, Apostle Al wanted to come to Congo, but he couldn't. As of the date that I am writing this, 2-09-08, they still don't have their passports. You can hear from the Lord, and still not listen.

> Today I met with Katembo Kiris, 50 Kitembo St. After a long song and dance I found out that Katembo wanted $100.00. He had nerve, there wasn't any real initial romance, he pretty much went straight for the money. They all think we are loaded down with cash, and it is theirs for the asking. Apparently other ministries come to Africa and throw money around or something. Well, Katembo showed his true colors early, not that he had a chance anyway, but after seeing that bold greed there was never going to be a chance in this lifetime.

Friday 8/1/08 8 am is the time the conference is scheduled in the little church. I didn't go because I was rounding up all of the sound equipment and was getting it ready for the revival. Things move slow here, and we got off to a slow start. We never did get the sound equipment set up for Edo at the morning conference. Her voice was torn up as a result. I got the sound equipment together and ready by 3pm or so – but I had a few technical problems due to the fact that I had never set up this particular brand equipment before. The bottom line was that when the guys showed up with the equipment we rented I had to make a call. I decided to use the equipment that we were renting from the locals rather than the equipment that we brought because I was under time pressure, and working equipment was better than nothing. The sound was absolutely awful – major distortion from the amps and speakers, buzz and hiss from the microphones, it was painfully bad. Edo was a trooper, and she marched on despite the difficulties. Around 2,500 to 3,000 people showed up. She gave her life story in her home town, and didn't name names this time. *At one point in her life she was married to a notorious murderer, and last time she named him. The family was upset, and word got back to her about it. Do you suppose anyone else in the family had that generational curse? (Edo is presently married to another man named Placide. He lives in London.)* Around 250 people gave their lives to Christ.

Saturday 8/02/08 This morning we worked on the generators before the morning conference. The little generator had a broken pull rope. It was a much bigger project to fix than met the eye because we had to find a rope somewhere. After taking the pull mechanism apart 3 to 4 times with the other mechanics, I gave up and left with the big diesel generator. The big generator had a cut fuel line, and there wasn't anywhere in town to buy a replacement. (remember that if it wasn't in town, the next town was 5 hours away) I have always known that the Lord has given me an amazing mind for understanding mechanical things. There really isn't anything that moves that I don't understand how it works. Additionally, I am extremely creative at ingenious repairs. I'm bragging on myself a little, but it is the truth. These skills come in so handy in the bush. I enjoy thinking of creative solutions to a problem. I found the same size line on the sweet little land rover and the problem was fixed in minutes.

We arrived at the conference with the sound equipment just as Edo was to begin speaking. Just in time. I realized that the sound equipment was one of the breaches that needed to be repaired, as the Crusade was called "Repairing the Breaches". Sometimes God's people needed to get their hands dirty to get the job done. I think it was a prophetic sign. The Lord was dealing with me on the foot washing experience. I didn't want to do it, but finally felt that souls could be saved, and people could be healed, so I released it at the morning conference. I then worked with the sound equipment until the revival started. The problem became that I got all the Amps and mixers hooked up and the sound quality was real nice. The "Other Guys" had equipment from the day previous, and they wanted to hook it up again. *I think they felt that they wouldn't make as much money if we ended up not needing their equipment. Their motivation was money, not seeing their friends and family set free by the Lord.* I was tired of the poor quality, so we butted heads the whole day. The bottom line was that we ended up using the same crap equipment today too, and the sound was awful again. I didn't even have the support of the musicians, apparently a little more volume with a ton of buzz and distortion was the only way to go in their minds. I finally gave up and went to get cleaned up at the goat hotel. Actually, I planned to use the good equipment while Edo was speaking, but the transition proved too difficult because there are no 9v batteries for the wireless microphone in the entire Congo. They had switched all of the regular microphones to the crap system. I was not feeling too happy because the entire process of getting the sound system working was aggravating. After getting cleaned up, I was finally able to return back to the conference.

Towards the end of her message, Edo told a few visions she had about people. Then she had them come up for prayer. She then spoke in Kicongo language and told them I had a vision, then had me come up and share it. I wasn't in the mood because I was quite tired, I had forgotten my Bible at the "Hotel" and I basically felt that it would be better to do it another time. There were 100 reasons not to go forward if you wanted one, but the wheels were already in motion, so I went. We got 3 benches and 10 cripples. I washed all of their feet, and prayed for them one by one, just like in the vision. I think a couple were totally healed, and several were significantly improved. One girl gave her life to the Lord. The whole thing took quite awhile, so at the end, we left.

Sunday am 8/03/08 It is now Sunday am, and I am still waiting for coffee. OK, so I was supposed to go to church this am while Edo was at the womans conference, but it turned out that there was some confusion, so Sunday was spent at the hotel.

I spent Sunday at the Hotel until time for the Revival. Around 4pm we left. The revival was good – Edo spoke on "Abide in Me" and it was good. I gave up on the sound system, and let it be the way that it was the last 2 days. It seemed that the attendance was low today, perhaps people were tired after attending their home churches. There were still more that 3,000 people at the revival, and there were so many children. I found out from Edo that the young girls go to the bigger cities to work as prostitutes. Then when they get pregnant, they drop the children with the parents here in Gungu. Around 600 people came forward to give their lives to Christ. The total attendance figures are amazing, as are the number of people coming to the Lord.

> *We all know that water baptism by immersion is a part of the conversion process. There was a logistics problem with so many people dedicating themselves at once, so the people were instructed to find a local congregation where they could be taught further. There was another issue concerning water baptism, and that is that some of the leaders of the various congregations were fighting about water baptism. The people that understood the importance of water baptism also tended to be very legalistic and controlling of their membership, even to the point of alienating and commanding alienation of those weaker in faith and understanding. We didn't want to get in the middle of this argument, or appear that we were taking sides.*

In order to understand the degree of legalism understand that Edo was wearing western womens conservative business attire, and some people had issues with it. I didn't have my collar button, or the next button buttoned on my shirt, and it bothered the legalists. I understand to a degree, but if a person dresses inappropriately and that becomes an issue right away, they may not stick around long enough to hear about Jesus. Lets meet them where they are, and then let the Holy Spirit teach them.

The people that didn't grasp the significance of water baptism yet were alienated from the legalists that did understand. This was because the legalists were all about obeying the rules, and those that had not been baptized yet hadn't obeyed the rules. It didn't matter to the legalists that they weren't at that point yet, what mattered was that they weren't obeying the rules. We are all at different levels, and if a person will honestly and humbly come to the Lord, He will meet them there and teach them what they need to know. The key is to diligently seek Him, and to press into His presence.

It was better for all concerned if we didn't publicly take sides on that issue at that time because that was not why we were there. Additionally, addressing the issue incorrectly would create more ammunition for the legalists. With all of the zeal that the legalists had about water baptism, I am sure that everyone had the opportunity to be baptized, once they understood it. Really, if someone is water baptized, and they don't understand it, they are really just getting wet, aren't they?

Monday 8/04/08 I found out this morning that we had a resurrection of the dead. While I was washing the feet of the lame and praying for them one of the lame girls sisters died. Her mother was a praying woman. She prayed for her daughter, and the Lord brought her back, praise God. See the video on Youtube, it explains a lot. http://www.youtube.com/watch?v=8zDqKVBvmBo

Today has been endless meetings with people that had various needs. The first meeting was with the previously dead girl, named Liddy. She looked to be about 18 or 20 years old. We prayed fervently for her, asking the Lord to continue to deliver her. We prayed for her and anointed her with oil. Afterwards she indicated that she felt much better, she also looked better, less oppressed, and more alive. It was a demonic oppression. Her mother said that she had moved from home, and was living with a room mate. Her room mate had taken Liddy's lotion and did something with it with a string wrapped around a bone placed in the lotion. I didn't get exactly what had happened, but it sounded like some kind of witchcraft. Liddy also indicated that she was sick with typhoid fever and pneumonia, or something like that. She was then treated at a clinic, and had gotten better. She returned home to Gungu with her two month old baby. Her baby then died, and Liddy became sick again. Thursday she got real sick and wouldn't eat. Then she began to vomit, and got very dehydrated. Apparently Saturday she died at home around the time I was praying for the lame. Her sister was one of the lame. Liddy's mother was praying for her, and I was praying for her sister at the same time. I prayed to have satan loose his grip on the lame girl, and her family. I commanded satan to leave the family alone, and broke all the curses off of the lame girl and her family in Jesus name.

The girl was dead for 30 minutes total, but she revived three times as verified by the attending nurse. After Liddy died, and while her mother was praying for her, Liddy came back to life and told the mother to stop praying. The mother said she did not recognize the voice, so she asked who it was. The voice said "Lucifer". Her mother then said "Lucifer, remember that Jesus won at the cross, so get out!" Liddy is with us today, able to walk and was doing much better, Praise God.

One of the pastors/musicians brothers that came with us got word that his brother had died in a car crash in Kinshasa, so he left with the translator this morning.

A man came by with tumors all over his face. He came to be prayed for. *They were large golf ball sized tumors all over his face ears and chin. What a burden to bear. His fiancée left him, and he was very unhappy. Additionally, he was a pastor, and people would tease him when he was evangelizing, making comments about the God he served, and his condition.* I felt the Lord told me to curse the tumors at the root and command them to die. He said after the prayer that he felt a cutting sensation at the base of the tumors after the prayer. *Sometimes people come for sympathy, or for money to cure their condition in the natural. They should come in faith, believing the healing power of Jesus.*

A woman came with a baby. The baby had hydroencephalitis, his head was very big and he was having some speech and hearing difficulties. We prayed for the intercessors as well. All of this activity, and it is not even lunch time yet.

People came with projects to be funded. They think that because we are from the developed world that we automatically have money. They had crude photocopies of business plans for a mechanics garage. There were only 5 cars in town, and 3 of them were ours. A hotel for missionaries, and a diabetic clinic. *It was like there was a guy down the street selling business plans to the people so they could present them to us. We accepted them graciously, and told them we would see what we could do. Then we put them in the pile of business plans. In case you haven't figured it out, there was no available funds, so they were wasting their time and ours. Additionally, even if I had it, I was not about to release money to someone I didn't know. Even some of the pastors were playing the money game. Did you know that the Lord would reveal the hearts of men if you ask Him? We are not blind. The Lord would show me things, for instance, once He showed me an empty fish hook. If you were stupid enough to bite on that one you would surely be hooked.*

I had a strange dream last night, although it was very vivid, the details are slipping. I was looking at heavy equipment-- I think it was Caterpillar. There was a lot of it. I went first to one place, and then to another. At the second place I accidentally backed my blue dodge truck off of a high seawall. The bed of the truck was in the water about a foot or two, but the truck wasn't damaged because it was hanging down by the bumper. I went to save it. Fortunately there was a woman that was going by in a bulldozer. I asked her to put the blade over by the bumper so I could chain the truck to the dozer. When she got close, she parked, and then suddenly engaged the dozer pushing the truck off into the water. I don't remember the details after that.

Tuesday 08/05/08 Today is the day we leave Gungu. The men started getting ready at daybreak. Edo and I had breakfast, and were underway by 8am. A short trip to the river and the ferry, then the wait to get three vehicles across. We missed the ferry when we arrived, so it was on the way across with some people on it, but no vehicles. On the other side they had to load a large all wheel drive truck. There were also a lot of boxes on the other side, heading for Gungu. Fortunately they were to be loaded at another time because it would have taken a long time to load them all up. After an hour and a half we were completely across, not bad. Edo told me the river was very deep, and in times past they had lost some of the large four wheel drive trucks in the river, but it was so deep and the water was so black, that there was no sign of the trucks.

While waiting, there was one of those dirty little roadside stands where they sell all kinds of foods and what not. This one had dirty little nuts on the stand. The nuts were covered with dirt, like they grew underground. According to Edo, they were Cola nuts. She explained that they bury them to keep them fresh. I wanted to try them, but they were covered with dirt. I remembered the open sewers and then imagined enough with that thought to prevent me from wanting them. Edo explained that we could wash them in the river. I had already been briefed about parasites in the water by a friend of mine in the US. She said don't even go into the water, let alone wash food in it. The knife they were going to use to cut the nuts was filthy as well. Later I remembered that we had drinking water in the Nissan, so I could have washed everything off, and felt safe. I was too busy being disgusted by the outward appearance to remember those things in the moment, so I just never did it.

After crossing the river by ferry, we drove on a jeep trail for awhile until we arrived in Kikwit. If memory serves, we were there by 1pm or so. There were people walking along the road all the way from Gungu to Kikwit. I don't know if they were going the whole distance, but it wouldn't surprise me. One pastor walked 80km to come to the revival so that he could invite Edo to come to his village. *Can you imagine? Walking close to 65 miles just for the opportunity to invite us to bring the Gospel to their village. The people in Africa are much hungrier for Jesus than the people in the USA. God help us.* We stopped by the hotel we stayed at in Kikwit so that we could pick up the chicken that we had left there tied to a table leg. He was still there, tied up after something like 5 days. The chicken survived the ride to Kinshasa, and was alive as of 8/8/08. The trip from Gungu was rough, but otherwise uneventful. Much better than the trip to Gungu, where we got stuck 5 times, and lost a muffler.

We bought more fuel in Kikwit, and headed off again towards Kinshasa. The road was paved, and we made pretty good time until around 10pm. We then stopped in a "city" and rested 2 hours. There were people wandering everywhere, sleeping on the sidewalks, it was a zoo. While resting I ate the first food since daybreak, canned sardines on sandy bread. *I have to add that I used to be seriously allergic to fish. Whenever I ate it in the past I used to get so so sick. My body would react violently, and all it wanted to do was get the fish out of me as fast as possible. I felt that I was healed in Lakeland, and to test it I ate a McDonalds's fish sandwich. If that didn't make me sick, I knew I was good to go. Thank God I was healed, because many times that is all there was.* There was a gay guy that greeted our vehicle when we stopped. He seemed particularly interested in talking with me. Needless to say that I was not interested. When in Africa everyone always targeted me from the scammers to the roadside salesmen. I was picked out of the crowd every time because they thought I had money. I knew that is why I was there, the Lord was using me to bring attention to the revival, it went with the territory, but it gets old. *Fortunately, I easily convinced this man that I wasn't interested in what he had, or what he was trying to accomplish.*

I was informed that the place we stopped was the end of the pavement, and that the trail was much worse from here on. I could not imagine roads much worse than what we were on, but that is what I was told. We paid a young man to show us where the jeep trail started. All of the vehicles were completely full, so he rode on the spare tire that was strapped to the back of SUV in front of us. Thank God he never fell off. It was several miles to where the trail started, the young man was paid, and then he walked back.

As soon as we got on the trail, the 4x4 got stuck, then got stuck again. Each time we got stuck, we were delayed while the men dug us out. We ended up getting stuck 5 times before we hit "good" trails again. The problem was that the enormous trucks that have a high ground clearance, and are 6 wheel drive and they cut giant 12" to 18" deep ruts through the sand. If the jeeps follow in their exact tracks, they don't have enough ground clearance to make it through the ruts without having the frame getting hung up in the sand. Since we were traveling at night, the trail was difficult to read due to the darkness. The jeep had to travel on either one side or the other of the truck trail. We had to constantly travel on either one side or the other of the truck trail, based on what the driver felt would be best to allow us to get through. This meant that we were constantly going across the deep ruts from the trucks. This made the road extremely rough, and to make it worse we had 9 people and the luggage jammed into a Nissan Terrano (similar to a pathfinder). I was in the second set of seats, next to the door on the left hand side of the vehicle with 4 people in a row designed for three. (The Nissan was from the UK and the drivers side was on the wrong side when compared to US vehicles). I was concerned about the door popping open and falling out, so I held on for dear life. By 2 am we had progressed only a few miles, barely staying in front of a big truck.

The big trucks set their diesels at about 2000 rpm's, kept the transmission in low and just crept along slow enough that a man could easily run as fast. I saw a man jump off of the back of the big truck we were just barely keeping up with, he then ran up to and caught the truck. He then pulled a long piece of bamboo out from under the truck, where it was stored. The truck remained at the same pace as he then ran up to the side of the truck with the bamboo pole, then just as the big truck was crossing the deep track they usually use, he threw the bamboo down lengthwise in the trucks path on one side so the truck could drive over it to gain some added traction. The big truck had to divert from the usual path in order to go around us. Obviously, this was a well rehearsed maneuver, because once the truck drove over the bamboo and the ruts, the man ran up to the bamboo, picked it up and replaced it on the truck. He then climbed back up on the truck, mission accomplished, and all in perfect rhythm without missing a beat.

The trucks went real slow, we barely kept up for two hours because of the terrain, and we kept getting stuck. Finally we got quite some distance from the truck. The Nissan I was riding in got stuck again, causing the muffler to fall off. This turned into an hour long midnight repair job that involved cutting the muffler clamps and placing a chunk of tailpipe in the rear seat.

We were off again into the night, bumping and pounding along from 12 am till daybreak. We still had not made it to Kinshasa. At some point in the night, the roads had gotten a little better because there was now some clay mixed in with the sand. The problem with the sand and the deep ruts was gone, but the roads were still rough, we were just able to travel faster.

We stopped again in the middle of the night in front of a hut. A small bamboo hut, just not as nice. People were sleeping on the ground in front of it. I couldn't see them because it was real dark, but I did hear a baby crying in their direction. They all got up and started moving around. I am not sure why we stopped, the road was blocked, or the ruts were too deep, or the muffler or something. I never did find out why we stopped, we were there for awhile, and I managed to sleep a little. The Land Rover was in front, but for the highway part of the journey, it was way behind. Once we hit the trails, it got way in front quick. We were off again. Later that night the musicians in the other SUV decided to stop because their clutch was slipping. Both SUV drivers were driving in the deep sand in 4WD high, rather than in low range. They really had to slip the clutch to get moving in the sand. The clutch finally got glazed, and started to slip all of the time. There was talk that they could not go on. There was practically no way we could pull them, and I don't think we had a chain to do it with. Fortunately, after a few minutes they decided that they were able to proceed. In no time they were way out in front, and now we were the last vehicle. Now our clutch started to slip, and we had to stay in 2nd gear. At least the road improved and was mostly paved.

It was at this point that my misery began. I was so careful to only eat cooked foods, and only drink bottled water. The only thing I could think of was the time we went to Edo's cousin Regine's house. They were all real nice, prepared a big meal. That is the first time I ate termites. I don't think it was the termites, I think it was the juice. I drank the juice, and I think I caught a bug. Since I wasn't used to it, it is easy to do. Anyway, the rumblings began. I knew what that meant. We were 2 hours from Kinshasa. I was afraid to start, because sometimes there is no stopping. The power of every bump, and every pothole was greatly magnified. I felt like I was going to explode. I was checking out bushes and looking for a safe place to go. The misery intensified every minute. Additionally, there was the motion sickness that was starting, and the associated headache. By this time I think it was around 2pm. That meant we had been traveling 30 hours with no stopping to speak of. My body ached from head to toe from the physical thrashing. My legs were so cramped up I couldn't sit still. I was miserable, but we made it to Kinshasa, relief must be close.

I thought we were going to stop at Edo's sisters house near town. It was the closest, and we drove right by. You know the anticipation when you think the misery is over, well the disappointment was enormous. I didn't want to let on about my problem, it wouldn't have helped because there were no gas stations, restaurants or public restrooms anywhere. I was looking everyplace, longing for a place to relieve the pressure. There was no hope in site. We were in the city now, people all around, there would have been witnesses to the carnage. No way to go, had to hold on. By now it was frighteningly painful. When we finally made it to Edo's sisters house, I rudely dashed to the restroom in front of everyone. I had no choice, this was an emergency of epic proportions. When I got to the restroom, the hall was dark, I couldn't find the handle, things wanted to happen so bad.... I made it, but it wasn't pretty. I tied up the bathroom for a long time. Others were feeling it too I'm sure. At least I made it. I didn't feel well that day, or the next. Regine was a nurse, so she was able to get some good medicine to plug me up. It wasn't till 8-8-08 that I started to feel better. I went to the internet that afternoon to tell the folks back home I was safe.

Wednesday 8-6-08 Today was just a lay around all day day. We went to the US embassy and checked in. We also went to Edo's husband Placide's office and used the internet. He is now in charge of telecommunications in the country, and his Boss is in charge of TV stations, like the F.C.C. is in the United States. Isn't it interesting that Edo is an evangelist, and all of the mass communication guys are right around her. We got home around 4pm. Did I mention we were out of money? Completely flat broke no cash at all, either one of us. Spent every dime on the revival. I gave some people in the US cash to hold so they could send it to me in case, and others had promised support. The bottom line was that I couldn't seem to communicate that I needed someone to immediately wire me some money. It didn't happen for 3 days. I ended up wiring myself $500 from the US by the internet. We got home too late to go to western union and get the money I wired myself.

Thursday 8-7-8 Today we went back to Placide Mukeza's office, (Edo's Husband) to pray concerning his new job, then we went to western union so I could get the $500 I sent myself. After picking up the $500.00, I checked my emails, and confirmed with the airlines concerning my departure. Evidently, if you don't tell them you are leaving, then you can end up bumped onto another flight. We then returned home, and my appetite had finally returned to the point where I wanted lunch.

Friday 8-8-08 I went to the internet to check on the money that was coming since we returned to Kinshasa. Unfortunately my friends in the US cannot figure out how to send it. I don't think they realize that if I was unable to send myself $500.00 that I would have been completely out of money since the 5th. Today was just a relax day. The big event was they picked up the Nissan and started to get the clutch replaced.

Saturday 8-9-08 I checked the internet again, they still have not sent any money. I called Pastor Al, he said that he is planning to come to the Congo. I sent him an email also so that he knows how to get hold of me. No other real news.

Sunday 8-10-08 We went to a church on the other side of town. Edo spoke mostly so it was nice, and in English :) churches are typically more interested in keeping their schedule than in following the Spirit. I felt that the Lord wanted to move in more signs and wonders, but time would not permit. The power was on for most of the day for a change. Pastor Jacque stopped by for a few minutes to say hello. He didn't stay long, and the trip to get there was a long one.

Monday 8-11-08 The mechanics are still working on the Nissan. Regine's brother Charlie stopped by.

Tuesday 8-12-08 The Nissan is finished. Things have been rather slow, we are mostly just hanging around the house watching everyone doing chores. I would really just be in the way if I tried to help, and labor costs are extremely low. I don't speak enough Lingala or French to hold a conversation, so I have been reading. Perhaps this is the source of the headaches. I finally broke down and bought some doxycyllin 100mg for the prevention of malaria. I was feeling achy, sweaty and sick to my stomach a little. I prayed to the Lord about it, and He removed some of the discomfort.

This is one of the dilemmas we face, I believe that the Lord will not only just send you to deliver His healing, but He will also prevent you from getting sick in the first place. "No plague shall come nigh my dwelling. " This is especially true if your primary focus is doing His works. However, my Mother is an extreme worrier about health. She expressly told me and basically made me promise to take medicine for malaria. We are to honor our parents, we are also to primarily seek the Great Physician for our medical care. So what is the answer? I sought the Lord over it and decided to go with His advice. Since my mother told me to take the malaria pills, and because the Lord also gave us common sense and He can heal through the doctors as well, it wasn't wrong for me to take the pills. It was not a compromise of my beliefs either because I sought Him and asked Him for direction first.

I decided to take advantage of the medical technology because being sick can be a serious problem. Malaria would knock me out for at least a week, possibly more based on what the medical professionals were saying. It is the old ounce of prevention thing.

Later on we went to the other sisters house, the one by the uncompleted tower. The children were there making gravel by hand. *Near this sisters' house there is an area where they make concrete blocks, and make big rocks into little rocks. The problem is that they use the labor of young children and old women. If you outlaw child labor, then these children would probably go hungry.* We also visited a pastor with a large uncompleted concrete church. We then drove past Regine's college, and the hospital to another Pastors house where we had lunch. Edo doesn't really trouble herself much to include me in the conversation. I see her point, it is difficult to handle so much. Like all of us, we have come a long way and there is still a ways to go. I am going to put it down as par for the course and let it go.

I ate pretty well today, something like four meals, pretty satisfying. The food for the most part is ok, it is just not what I am used to.

I have been mentally stuck on Adam in the Garden coupled with the redemptive healing work of Jesus on the cross for the past few days.

Because we have never fully experienced what Adam had, we don't realize what we lost when he fell. Christ is our healer "As Moses lifted up the serpent in the wilderness" Medicine sometimes uses a little poison like what is afflicting us to cancel another disease, like a vaccine.

Wednesday 8-13-08 Nothing really going on. I'm at the house, and I feel pretty good. Regine is doing my laundry by hand. Socks and underwear, the jeans are too heavy for her. I need to go to western union to get the $800 today. *It finally arrived. Special thanks to Apostle Al Davis and Consuming Fire International Ministry. The money was spent back in Kikwit blessing all of the ushers (120 +/-) for their 3 days labor every day at the revival. Do the math, these folks are hard pressed anyway, and now they had to take time off work to help out. It worked out to about $6.00 each for three days work.*

Edo had a dream about cleaning up the poop at her sisters sugar depots. We went around to all three of her stores and anointed the stores with oil and prayed over them. I got some weird visions while praying at the stores. A pin wheel, a steel bridge across a canyon, a cotton candy machine, and a mason jar with a steel scoop on one end, full of sugar. I don't understand them. At one of the stores I saw a pagoda type building with a small cross on it, but it was short, like an x turned on its side. The only help on the vision was that there was a Jehovah's Witness that worked there. The pagoda was like a false religion. Hmmm

We then went to some Pastors big house. He was preparing for the evening lesson, so he couldn't see us. We then went downtown to a big store. The beggars were everywhere along with the street peddlers. We then went to the fabric market. They had lots of interesting prints I bought one with Jesus on the cross printed on it. The fabric sellers didn't seem to get the difference between Jesus and Mary. They kept showing us prints with Mary on it. When we finally arrived back home, the power was out. When it came back on, I went to the internet store. The internet again proved to be unreliable because the connection was on and off. You can spend an hour composing an email, only to have the power go off in the middle, losing your work. Even if you save it, since it is not your computer, there is no guarantee you can come back to the same machine and get your work. Thus, run around Wednesday is complete.

Thursday 8-14-08 Apparently the next service we do is ear night. I was half awake, half asleep this morning and I saw a funnel sideways with a membrane slipped over the big end....an eardrum. Then, a short while later it was a pipe all curled up, ok so it was the inner ear thing. Modern art meets the medical journal. I then saw the congregation. All the way back on the right hand side by the aisle there was a deaf woman. She was probably deaf in both ears because they had to escort her to the stage. *That is what I wrote, but for the life of me I can't imagine what that has to do with both ears being deaf, if she was blind, I could understand it.* She was 40 to 50 years old, and was wearing a dark blue and orange or red accented African dress with a head scarf that matched. She looked thin and worn. When she came up, I verified her condition, then I rebuked the deaf and dumb spirit. I placed my hands over her ears, she fell out and then started crying, shocked that she could hear. The impression I got was that it was the first time in her life that she could hear. Then the Lord opened it up for ears, I felt that there were no deaf ears left in the congregation. I also felt that her name had an "M" in it like Mary. (Her name was actually "Mado(line)") She was deaf in one ear, and God healed it.

Today seemed like it was going to be a hang around the house type day, then Edo said that the pastor we were trying to meet Wednesday was waiting for us. We waited around for the man called Pastor Jude, he had tried to introduce us to Pastor Roland Dalo Wednesday. Anyway, Dr. Jude was late, but it was no problem. *Pastor Jude was a busy man. He was always running a tight schedule, therefore he was usually running late. He was a wonderful man that opened the door to many churches for us. May God Bless him and his family for all of the faithful service he did for the Kingdom.* We finally met Dr. Jude at the gas station around the corner. I drove to Roland Dalo's house. It was the first time I drove since we arrived in the Congo.

Driving in the city in Congo is a terrifying experience. There are no real laws on how to drive, the laws are merely suggestions. If you did get into an accident, you were expected to argue with the other driver and settle things without the benefit of police intervention. If the police did show up, they basically decided guilt or innocence on the spot and levied fines as well. The guilt or innocence and the fines were based on the connections and the pocketbooks of those involved. People drove on the wrong side of the road, they swerved across the center without notice to avoid potholes and craters, their vehicles were in serious disrepair. Pedestrians were everywhere. Vehicles never stopped for pedestrians, so watch where you walk. It was Bedlam. I am an excellent professional driver in the US, this place was nuts to drive in. The roads were not marked, people just had to know the way. It was a stressful experience to say the least. All I needed was to have someone hit us, and then end up getting tattooed by the authorities here. My sister had an experience like that in another country, a man jumped in front of her, and then the police took her passport and wouldn't let her leave. It was an expensive mess to get out of.

Roland Dalo had a nice big house. They had a newer Audi and a Mercedes in the driveway. A large house, a well manicured lawn, God was good to Roland Dalo. Roland spoke English, which was nice. We waited for him about 20 minutes, and then the meeting lasted for about 20 minutes. We just told him about ourselves, and about Edo's ministry.

After the meeting, I told him about the vision I had while praying at his house. I asked him if he had an anniversary coming up. He told me that he did have on October 18th. In the vision that I had, I saw a beautiful black lady and she was being given a heavy gold necklace with a single gold pearl on it. The pearl was like a pendant. She was real happy, then I saw them happy together, and celebrating their anniversary and their togetherness. Pastor Dalo said that this was perfect because he was wondering what to get his wife for their anniversary. God is interesting, he gave me the gift idea, and I released it not knowing the meaning. Now his wife will be happy which will surely give us great favor with this man of God and his ministry. I get credit for the gift in both of their minds, and I didn't have to pay a dime. I think that it meant more than if I had bought the necklace, especially since he can now tell anyone who asks the story of the vision, and it takes away any accusations of extravagance.

After meeting with Pastor Dalo, we went to the 15 story government office building that housed the water department offices. We met and prayed with the man who is in charge of the water and the electric for the entire country. His department has received a $15 million dollar grant to study the hydroelectric potential in the Congo. I told him that the Lord showed me to take some of the money and build a small working model so they could base their report on real world conditions. As a working model, it could be used to give tours and demonstrate the effectiveness thereby producing good P.R. and political points.

After the meetings, we then returned home. The school children are graduating today, so they were really celebrating. They were hooting and hollering, blowing whistles, and dousing each other with talc. It was funny to watch. The children were also stacked up 100 deep at the internet store, so it would not be possible to get access for pretty much the whole day.

The hydroelectric has been on my mind since I found out about the Congo trip. *I learned very early on that the Congo was a net exporter of hydroelectric power, distributing power as far away as Egypt and South Africa. The Congo has 10% of the worlds hydroelectric potential. A vast and powerful economic resource.* Funny how the Lord works, putting me in the correct office. I have met one of the most influential pastors in Kinshasa, The man in charge of all of the hydroelectric power for the country, The man in charge of Television and Radio licensing, who was also best friends with Edo's husband Placide Mukeza. *Putting it all together it sounds like the power and the licensing to put the Gospel on the airwaves is available, doesn't it? God is able, isn't He.*

Friday 8/15/08 There is a conference tonight at 5 pm. Its ear night. No other visions or words. That will be enough by its self. Well, it turns out funny. The lady that had the ear problem left early, so it didn't happen tonight. Her daughter was still there, she said that her mother would be back Sunday when we returned. Interesting world. Edo spoke and gave her life story, and the people really liked the message and they responded well to it. The sound system had the same problems in this church that they had everywhere else. Poor sound quality seems to be an epidemic here.

As far as the deaf woman is concerned, sometimes we come into church and into the presence of the Lord with a plan in our minds, and sometimes I think we miss His will for us. I'm not exactly sure how all of that works out, I just know He is busy working things out for us. I believe that in time, and as we grow He will be revealing more to us.

Saturday 8/16/08 Today Edo's niece named Tender is supposed to show up to take me to see the Bonobo Chimpanzees that are native to only the Congo. *I referred to her as the "Monkey Girl" when I first heard about the plans, but that turned out to be very unpopular. I was really just kidding around (monkeying?) but it was not well received. I really wanted to see the chimps, because I really think monkeys are cute and funny.* I spent the morning attempting to repair the window in the Nissan. The window had fallen out of its track, and wouldn't go up and down. I worked out a repair that worked real good for a few hours, then the window mechanism broke again. Nice try.

Tender showed up a little late, right in the middle of my window project, so I hurried up and got things wrapped up. We soon departed to see the Bonobo monkeys (but actually they are chimpanzees) *Tender went to a lot of trouble to take me to see the chimps, she borrowed a car from her work, or actually rented one, with a driver. I'm not sure how it worked, but it seemed real nice for her to go to that much trouble. She was very nice also, and was quite educated and fluent in English.* The Bonobos were very cool and quite tame. They did all of the usual monkey stunts much to my amusement. I had a very nice time.

The Bonobos are in a preserve that is quite resort like. It was very well maintained and was the very nicest place I had been to in the Congo. With the exception of the guards with automatic weapons, it was very much more like a western resort than anyplace else in the Congo. They had a restaurant, and we got a table under a cabana near a waterfall overlooking the beach. There were some Europeans there with their children. The children were young, and were running all over the beach naked as jaybirds. It was cute and funny. We ordered lunch at the restaurant, but it took forever to prepare. It was ok because we were having a nice conversation. It was a nice lunch, very pleasant and enjoyable, even though we did end up running late. Edo was speaking this evening, and we had the Lord's work to do. Just to add to the pressure, we were a little late getting home, which in turn made us late getting to the church. By the time I got back home, we had to leave quickly and return back nearly to the place where the Bonobo preserve was located. The church was also located near to the church where I had the vision about the ears. Since I don't speak the local lingo, and the streets aren't marked well, it is difficult to tell where we actually are. Sorry about that.

Sunday 8/17/08 Up early, and off to Pastor Roland's church. The service was real nice, and the presence of the Lord was the strongest I had felt in any church in the Congo so far. We left about 9:30 and headed to a church that was at the bottom of a hill near the house where we were staying.

The hill was very steep, and today there was a Chevy truck that was up on blocks that had had an accident coming down the hill. Perhaps his brakes failed, and he lost control and headed into the ditch. On the side of the road, they had poured a curb out of concrete, about every three feet there was a space in the curb so the water could flow into the ditch. The truck had jumped the curb and then really messed up the suspension on the curb. They were now in the process of fixing it right there. This was very common in the Congo, I saw many, many vehicles being repaired on the roadside. People probably get run over that way all the time, but no one seems to care. This is like America in the early 1900's when there were no liability laws or consumer protection. It was like the wild west, because there were not strict enforcement of laws like there is in the States.

I digress, Edo shared her life story again, we had a couple of words of knowledge, I had a few closing comments, and the closing prayer. *The people respond in a funny way to the gospel in the Congo, no one wants to be first, but after the ice is broken, they come in droves. I think the words of knowledge function in a similar fashion. The Lord calls you out to handle a situation in your life, be it a healing, or a word of encouragement or correction, and the people are shy to respond. I understand it to a point, but really the Lord has good things for them, and again no one moved. By this time we have had so many positive results through words of knowledge, that it is hard to imagine people too shy to get their blessing.*

After church we went home and rested up for the evening service. This evening we were at the "ear" church again. After Edo spoke about the presence of the Lord, I spoke on healing a few minutes and called for the ear lady again. Once again, she wasn't there. This was getting comical. We had to go because Edo was also scheduled to speak at the church at the bottom of the hill in the "Mama Mobutu" neighborhood. This was the neighborhood to live in when Mobutu was in power, plenty of nice big houses. Edo spoke the whole message in Lingala. I knew it wasn't Kicongo because they didn't predominantly speak that language in this region. I was basically lost, having no idea what she was talking about. The people were all very cordial, and we prayed for a bunch of them.

During the service, since I couldn't follow the sermon, I engaged the Lord in prayer. He showed me a vision of a large, deep, hand dug well that had a ring shaped rock and mortar top. It was about three feet across. I saw a bunch of thirsty, hungry African children around the well. I then remembered the woman at the well in Johns Gospel, and the verse "You have nothing to draw with, and the well is deep." I realized that the well was the church, and the water was the Lord. The church was not thirsty because it could draw the water. The people around the church were thirsty. The church was supposed to teach those around it how to draw the water. I shared the vision and the interpretation with the church.

After we left the church, I was told that we were going to stop at the ear ladies house. Edo had a word of knowledge for her also about worshiping the Lord. I didn't really know what to expect at this point because I had had such a detailed word of knowledge for this woman, and I had no idea that the Lord was going to move at her house instead of the church. The scenario didn't exactly match the vision I had, but I was still going to go along with it. I wasn't the one doing the healings, just the vessel. It was a good thing that Edo had already set everything in motion, because I had already figured that she had missed her day of visitation, and her blessing. There is a lesson in this for all of us. After the introductions, I asked her if she believed that Jesus could heal her ear, and she answered "yes". I then asked if she believed He would heal it now, and she said yes again. I then placed my hands over her ears, like I saw in the vision, prayed and rebuked the devil, the spirit of infirmity, the deaf and dumb spirit, and commanded the ears to be healed. When I prayed earnestly everything I could think of, I removed my hands, and snapped my fingers. She indicated that her ear was healed. Her response was very calm, without much excitement, but that she was healed. I asked if the ears were the same, in other words if the volume levels were the same in both ears. She indicated that they were not, so I prayed again for good measure. She was healed after being deaf for 8 years in one ear, her left. Praise God. She made a donation to the ministry in dollars and Francs that totaled around $40.00. This was a large contribution considering the local economic condition. We spent it all on gas almost immediately, but it helped. I am thankful that she had a gift for the ministry, and perhaps that was the point of it all. I don't really know, it was so unusual for me. God healed her, and we got some help along the way. Amen.

After we got home we ate buffalo, which was very good, and then I went to sleep, and slept like a rock.

Monday 8/18/08 Today was a day off, but I managed to fill it with interesting activities. I went on the Great Glue search. I was looking for Liquid Nails in order to fix the window on the Nissan.

> *Did I ever tell you that things are different here? :) They distribute products differently here. Most "stores" are little 10x10 shanties with different items in them. Some areas of town specialize in furniture, or lumber, or used auto parts, or what not. It is like that, instead of a big retailer locking down a product line, various neighborhoods will specialize in certain things. There are other stores thrown in for good measure, but most of them are as I described.*

Well, good luck with the glue search. Between the language barrier, the limited distribution of many products that are common in the States it wasn't happening. *I went with Elijah, Ellie for short, and we walked all over the place for several hours, going from store to store. He didn't speak English, and the store owners mostly didn't either. We finally found some silicon glue, once they understood what I was looking for. Liquid nails would have been ideal, but the silicon glue would work.*

Today was a day off, and I wanted to go to the internet later on. Once I found the glue, and fixed what I wanted to fix, I started to head that way, then the power went off. Just to make it interesting, sometimes the power would go off on our street, but the internet stores would have power, and other times they wouldn't. The best thing to do was to walk the 10 minutes, and go check. I ended up working on the spark plug wire and the window of the Nissan. One cylinder in the Nissan was missing, and overall the power was low. It turned out that one of the spark plugs had a bad wire. You couldn't buy one wire, you had to look all over, and they would sell you a used set. I took the wire apart and re-clamped the old ends of the wire, and that fixed the sparking problem. It helped the power problem a little, but it didn't fix it. I think that since that cylinder didn't get a good spark, the gasoline washed out the rings, and the rings needed to be replaced. That was more project than I wanted to tackle. Fortunately labor is cheap, but quality workmanship and integrity are another matter.

8/19/08 Up early and the Nissan won't start. Edo and I tried to bump start the Nissan, but with no success. The Nissan was hard to start when it was cold anyway. I switched the batteries with another vehicle and got it started. I then switched the batteries back. We got the Nissan running, and ended up going to Lemba to spend the day with Edo's Sister.

> *This entire experience has been one of amazing spiritual growth. I would like at this time to thank everyone involved in the revival for the grace and understanding extended towards me as necessary due to offenses I may have unknowingly committed due to cultural misunderstandings and differences. It is exceedingly difficult to fully understand and fit into a new culture right away. We all still have feet of clay. There is always the possibility of issues that come up that require special grace. We can experience difficulties that can arise due to the rigors and stresses of travel and these stresses can affect our relationships. Thank you Jesus for the grace and understanding of others that was extended towards me, and I thank Jesus for the grace to extend this to others.*

8/20/08 Today is looking like one of those lay around all day type days. It seems like there have been too many of those the past few weeks.

> *This is work in a sense, working for the Lord. Your emotions can be all over the place. Sometimes it is quietly enjoying the presence of the Lord, other times it is holding dying babies. Nice and peaceful, then surrounded by lots of people in severe need of medical help. Things swing from one extreme to the other pretty quick.*

The phone rings, it is Dr. Jude. We had a meeting that he forgot to tell us about. We went to a little church with a dirt floor (So far only two churches had concrete floors.)in Lemba near the tower and Pastor Jacks church.

Edo gave her testimony, then we prayed for everyone that wanted to receive Christ as their savior, then since only 70 to 75 people were present, we prayed for everyone there. The church leadership was cool, they told us to take all the time we wanted. It was a nice church, people kept coming all through the service. While Edo was speaking, I was engaging the Lord in prayer. He was showing me that a big increase in souls was coming. First I saw a large sheath of wheat, then I saw a big net full of fish. I understood that the Lord was showing me that a big harvest was coming.

One of the ladies I prayed for needed a healing in her legs and knees. I was praying in English, then I asked her to do something she couldn't do before. As I prayed and said these things and before the translator could translate, the spirit of the Lord hit her and she began jumping all around. I thought that she was going to fall out in Gods presence, but she didn't.

Really it wasn't all that interesting, I just mentioned it because there is no way that she understood what was going on, except that she knew she was being prayed for. Then, without her knowing what I am saying, the Spirit of the Lord hits, and she starts hopping all around. It is just interesting.

I prayed for a bunch of ailments, although I believe there were some healings, I just don't remember anything instant, or substantially notable.

A woman did come to the church with a picture of a boy that was in a coma. We laid hands on the photo, and asked the Lord to heal the boy. Later, we learned that the woman that brought the picture reported that the boy awoke after we prayed over the photo. Praise God.

Thursday 8/21/08 Once again we laid around the house all morning, around 4pm we left for another church, The Mount of Transfiguration. It wasn't too far from Lemba. One of the speakers was sick, so they asked Edo to come and fill in. She spoke on Moses, and the time his face shone so much, he had to wear a veil. I got the message through a translator, so I may have missed most of it in the translation. At the end of the night, Edo asked if I had anything to say. I asked how much time we had, she indicated that we had enough. I released that the Lord wanted to do miracles, it was actually a big night for miracles. He reminded me of the deaf woman, and the man with the tumors. He also reminded me of the gold dust and the gold teeth, but we never got that far. Interestingly enough, Edo woke up early this morning covered with gold dust all over one arm.

I released the deafness, and the tumors and no one moved. The Congolese move so slowly. Anyway, ultimately 35 to 50 people came forward. One lady had a tumor on her feet, I prayed for her, then laid one hand on her tumor while cursing the tumor and commanding the tumor to dry up and fall off. I was praying in English without being translated, the Spirit of the Lord hit her, and she fell out on the floor, and laid there a few minutes. I also prayed for a young boy there that was about 9 years old. I asked him if he was a member of the church, and if he knew Jesus to which he answered yes. He indicated that he was deaf in one ear, I asked him if he believed Jesus would heal him right now...he said yes. I then prayed for his ear, rebuking the deaf and dumb spirit in Jesus name. When I was through, we tested his ear and it was opened. Praise God! A mother was there, she had a young son that was about 2 years old. He was also deaf in one ear. I prayed for him also, when we tested his ear he answered his mother when she spoke into his previously deaf ear. Thank You Jesus. I also prayed for a woman in her 50's that was deaf in one ear, it was opened also.

There were women with reproductive troubles, people with financial difficulties, various maladies that needed to be dealt with. So many times there is no outward sign of a healing, but the Spirit of the Lord is still at work. One girl was wearing a red shirt. *Not that it mattered, but I didn't know her name or anything about her, so the red shirt is how she is now identified.* She indicated that she has stomach troubles, and an oppression of some kind. *There seems to be a mild epidemic of people suffering from stomach troubles. I am sure that it is closely related to diet and sanitation.* As I was praying for her, she indicated that she felt like she was going to vomit. We got her a bucket, and I kept praying. I couldn't get whatever it was that was ailing her to come clear out, so I asked Edo to help. After a short while, I was called off to pray for someone else while Edo continued to pray for her deliverance. At the end of the night, Edo gave the report of what had happened to the Pastor, so he asked for testimonies. One woman testified that she felt the power of God and electricity or something similar. I believe I was the one who prayed for her knees. No one else testified, I think they are too shy. I know that at least two people had their ears opened. There was also a woman that had cataracts healed. It would be really cool to be an eye specialist in the Holy Ghost. This pretty well concluded the service for the night. We really need someone to write down all of the testimonies to document what the Lord did after a healing service.

Friday 8/22/08 Up early as usual, then nothing pressing all morning. I decided to go to the internet store and send an email. When I got there the power was out, so that wasn't going to happen. Friday was supposed to be a day off. I became lax in my note taking and didn't write the events of Friday until the following Monday.

We went to the Catholic Church from 7pm until 10 pm Friday night. It struck me as a long service for a Catholic service, plus it was "pentecostal". The church is still Catholic because they are very strict on their own interpretation of who they say Mary was. The Pentecostal that they did was not with signs and wonders following, it was just a less somber service than what they would traditionally do. Edo said that they would send people out to other non catholic churches to take sermon notes, and basically to spy out the territory. Edo also said that they even asked her for her notes, which she said that she was happy to give them. I see her point, then they can come to a better knowledge of the truth. The service seemed very familiar. As had become my habit during long sermons where I didn't understand the language, I just engaged the Lord in prayer. The only difference was that in this particular instance, it was very difficult to get into the Throne Room, His presence and focused. When I finally did get in I had a vision of a large white leafy fungus with a small candle growing in the middle. The fungus was unclean, and the candle was a small light. I think it was accurate, but I prefer visions where I don't know anything going on that might influence it. The service didn't seem very Catholic at all. A chameleon changes colors.

If you are going to church in Congo, and especially at this particular church, you need to bring your own chair. Almost everyone had a plastic chair on their head. Edo's sister had already sent someone ahead with the chairs, so we didn't have to carry them, and they were waiting for us when we arrived. This was also the case at the revival that we held. There were hundreds of people walking down the road carrying chairs on their heads.

Saturday 8/23/08 Today we went to Regine's (Edo's cousin) church in Ndelli, near the little Kinshasha airport. It was a small church of 75 persons or so. It was reported earlier that there were some immorality problems in the church body, and there was also the possibility of a faithfulness issue with the leadership between a husband and a wife. The wife was running around and wanted to come back, meanwhile, the husband was having an affair with a woman at another church he oversaw in another city. All rumors at this point, but there has to be something to it somewhere, so we knew we were going into a mess. We showed up and everything seemed to be ok, I was able to enter into the Kings presence ok. I sensed an oppression. The worship was loud, and a little rowdy.

Sometimes we are in disobedience, so we do things to cover it up so no one will notice. It is like turning up the car radio so you cannot hear the motor making noise, so people will turn the music up louder so hopefully no one will notice that the Spirit isn't there. People will carry on in sin all week, and then make sure they praise the Lord extra vigorously to make up for it.

Edo gave her testimony, the same one that people always responded to in droves. In this particular church, no one moved. It was a painful pregnant pause that to me indicated some deeper spiritual issues. Finally, Dr. Jude came up and spoke a few minutes then 20 to 30 people came up for prayer. As I was praying for someone, a woman came forward and said that she was having trouble with her eyes. I didn't really understand, so I got the translator. He said that the womans right eye wasn't working properly, she had a dark spot in her vision. It would have been something like a detached retina or macular degeneration. I prayed for her eyes, and when I was through, she indicated that her vision was better. As she went to sit down, I asked her through the translator if her vision was 100%. She indicated that it was better, but not 100%. I prayed for her some more, and then she said it was completely healed. Praise God.

A little later another lady came forward with a bad right eye also. I prayed for her, but her vision only improved slightly, or not at all. I asked her to come back Sunday. The Spirit of God moved throughout the night, and we made some headway. That night I asked the Lord about it, so I could know what was happening. I would spit in her eye like Jesus did if I was sure He was telling me to do it. I felt I needed to anoint her with oil and press in some more. I spent hours on behalf of the blind lady, but I never did see what the problem was.

Sunday 8/24/08 We were back at the little church in Ndelli, and I was feeling the spirit of oppression pretty heavy now. Once I entered in, I realized that the people were living however they wanted to, and then were trying to worship like crazy to cover it up. Edo essentially covered the same ground in her message, so I didn't really see the point in releasing it again. Edo's message was almost entirely in Lingala :(so they were getting scolded, and I didn't catch much of it. At the end of the message, we had them come up for prayer. The prayer started out tame, but quickly got real wild. Edo and I were both praying for people that had dropped to the floor because of the power of God. Additionally, there were some serious deliverances taking place. One of these was a sweet looking 12 to 13 year old girl who came forward for prayer. So sweet and innocent looking, pray for me. Once I began prayer she fell to the ground and began writhing all over the place, arching her neck and her back. She was finally carried behind a curtain and was prayed over for 30 to 45 minutes. All told, three or four people were carried behind the curtain for more deliverance and prayer. *It was warfare with the enemy. If the laying on of hands stopped, the people being prayed for would calm down and quit moving, as soon as Edo or I would touch them again they would begin writhing and flopping around again as a reaction to our touch. It was the Spirit of the Lord at work.*

Most of the congregation stayed all morning. That was pretty good. At the end of it all, I asked the formerly blind in one eye lady to give her testimony. The church loved it. I then brought the other lady up that was blind in one eye as well. I had the church pray for her, and I anointed her with oil and laid hands on her. I could see the improvement, but the eye didn't heal instantly. She said that the pain had left. I couldn't seem to get through to the results that I wanted, I had to keep stopping because the church wasn't really praying. I told them to pray, as I was really pressing in. It just wasn't enough. I should have prayed for her 7 times like Elijah did because I wanted to see a complete healing right then. Healings don't come the way we expect they should. They can be instant, or they can happen over time. This lady did show some remarkable improvement. I didn't hear how it all ended, but I thank God for the major healings and deliverances that we did have.

After the service, I asked the translator to go get the formerly blind lady so I could get her testimony on video. He didn't seem to get it, so I asked him to ask Regine to do it for me, and she acted like she didn't want to. I am sure there was a translation or understanding problem. It is funny because people are always doing things they think are important, but that I don't particularly need done. Like washing my walking shoes, or carrying my Bible. Then when there is something that is important to me, like getting a glass of water, or in this case getting the formerly blind in one eye lady's attention, it doesn't happen. It was mostly a cultural thing, coupled with translation problems. The video turned out very poorly due to the background noise and the translation problems. It is also available on youtube. http://www.youtube.com/watch?v=Oc2Wmjdfz7M

Monday 8/25/08 I still have not heard from Pastor Al. Supposedly he was coming to the Congo. We went to Brussels Airline so that Edo could check for a possible early departure. There were some issues that she needed to address in London at the home front. There was no way that was going to happen, there just were no available seats on any airplanes leaving for London. While we were out, we stopped by the tailor shop as well to check on the progress on the shirt and dress we were having made for Apostle Al Davis and his wife Dorothy. Unfortunately the shop was already closed for the day.

When we arrived home, I wanted to go to the internet store to check my email. Marcel was at the house waiting for us to arrive. He was the man that I had met earlier that spoke English. Marcel decided to go with me to the internet store. I am sure that it was boring for him because we were there for 45 minutes. He was nice about it, and it did give him a good chance to practice his English with a native speaker. After spending some time together, we went back to the house. When we arrived, his friend the "Pastor" was there waiting for us. I sent a runner to the store to purchase a Coke or a Maltina for anyone that wanted one. After we sat around and socialized awhile, they took off then we had dinner. *Interestingly enough, a Coke or a Maltina only cost 200 francs. Since the exchange rate was 550 francs for a dollar, the drinks cost less than twenty cents apiece. Maltina is a sweet malt based beverage somewhat similar to non alcoholic beer.*

Tuesday 8/26/08 Today we spent all day praying for people. Around 10 am we went to the building next to the church that was down the hill that was within walking distance of Edo's sister's house. It was the same hill where where the Chevy truck crashed coming down the hill, and ruined the front end. We worshiped awhile, Dr. Jude gave a sermon in Lingala, then prayed for everyone present. I think they were all intercessors, there were nearly 100 altogether. I got the line for people that wanted some kind of healing in their bodies. I had no way of knowing what they needed healed, so I sought the Lord, and prayed as he lead me. It got real wild, and the prayer was very intense. I got real sweaty, we were all upstairs in a small room, so it was real hot, and we all were soaked. People were occasionally falling out under the power of God. There was also a lot of resistance. It is funny, its like when people decide they are not going to fall out under any circumstances, so they resist and fight. I guess they feel they will appear weak. When I get a chance, I will try to teach them to just relax and receive what the Lord has for us.

Afterwards we went to the church where the woman attended that got healed of deafness by a word of knowledge. Again Edo spoke, and again it was in Lingala. I had a word of knowledge about a woman who was about 45 or so years old, who had recently lost her husband. About 1 or 2 months ago. I also saw a little girl playing with a small stuffed animal. The stuffed animal looked like a dog. I felt that the little girl was the same woman, and that the Lord was restoring her joy. I released the word, and sure enough, the woman was there.

> *Now what are the odds that a woman would be there in a crowd numbering less than 100, and that she would have lost her husband in the last few months? It is possible that it was just a random lucky guess, but we all know better, don't we.*

This woman was already whacked by the Holy Ghost because we had already prayed for her once. She came forward and got it again. When I told Edo about the toy, the interpretation became that the Lord wants to restore your joy. I feel that this was very accurate, because the toy was like a favorite toy that she had when she was little, and the Lord wanted to encourage her. I really didn't take the time to probe into the story surrounding the toy. I am sure that there were some additional details, but you can only do so much. I also didn't have time to get the details about who she lost and so on.

After we finished at this church, we went to the large church that had the upstairs office. It is the one that was doing the "Mount of Transfiguration". They had a big banner that said "Mount of Transfiguration" on it, the funny thing was that the mountain pictured on the banner was the Matterhorn. If I remember correctly, Jesus never climbed or was never transfigured on the Matterhorn. :)

Edo spoke on tactics of spiritual warfare. Again mostly in Lingala, again I spent the time in prayer. I saw a factory in a vision. The factory was turning wooden spindles on lathes. I don't know, someone must be getting a blessing that works in that field. I then saw an injured right hand, perhaps it was a healing. The word was never released because they were on a strict program or schedule.

We prayed for a woman that had high blood pressure. She was healed. She went to the doctor and had it checked and then reported it this evening, Praise God.

> *It is like that sometimes, the most important thing to people is to stay on the schedule. The reality is that the most important thing is to follow the Spirit of the Lord. Sometimes the local church leaders can get envious also. The people can wonder why their leaders don't operate in signs and wonders, thus creating a question about their leaders walk with the Lord. Different ministries have different purposes. People that travel have a different calling than those that have a located ministry. We should not envy one another, rather we must work together because we each have things the other person needs.*

It is now well past dark. We head home for the first meal of the day, except for the four pieces of toast I had for breakfast.

Wednesday 8/27/08 I felt that something was wrong. I couldn't put my finger on it, it was just a sense of trouble or danger. My grandmother is 89 years old, and living in a nursing home. It was like there was trouble there. I did what I could, I covered it in prayer until I felt better. I wanted to go to the internet this morning, but the power is out.

I finally got eggs for breakfast! I have been so hungry from time to time here. Yesterday, I basically didn't eat all day, then we ate late. The dinner was in my stomach like a rock. At least I ate, Thank You Jesus. I saw so many children that must have gone to bed hungry. My stomach shrank, and it was difficult to get enough sometimes. I woke up hungry, and the eggs were very welcome. No other real news today. I am just waiting for the power to come back on so I can check email. We are going back to the "Mount of Transfiguration" this evening for part two.

Also, I didn't write it down, but I got a vision of the big Vodacom stadium in Kinshasa being used for a revival. I felt that it would be in the second week of August 2009. I also saw free Bibles and food being distributed for everyone. The vision was on Monday night Aug 25th. I am going to tell the translator about it and find out the details for making a deposit.

At 5:30 pm we were at "The Mount of Transfiguration" Edo spoke for an hour and a half in Lingala. This church is really into religion because they have a rigid pattern of worship. Edo spoke, then she called for people to be prayed for. She asked me to pray for the people along with Dr. Jude. The first group of people we prayed for was women that had a fiancée but the fiancée couldn't decide to get married. I didn't figure out what we were praying for until I had already prayed for at least two of them. God already knew, and they didn't speak English, so I don't suppose it mattered. There were quite a few women that came forward. Afterwards, we prayed for the men who couldn't decide. To come forward would have been a real show of weakness for the men. And if their girlfriends were there and they were spotted being indecisive, then they would have been in real trouble I suppose. One man did come forward to be prayed for, so I prayed for him. I had asked Edo the night previous if we were going to have the opportunity to lay hands on and pray for everyone. I like to do it, especially for healings. It really depends on the church that we are visiting. Some will allow you to run late, others won't. Since we were running late, Edo handed the microphone to the head Pastor, and that was pretty much the end of it for the night. Nevermind. The fact is that I had a word of knowledge that I felt needed to be released but it just couldn't happen.

It is a learning experience. I had been with a ministry called "Consuming Fire International Ministry" in Sarasota, Florida. We were blessed that there was freedom in the house, and it was never about ending on time, rather it was about what the Lord was doing. It was a little loose and strange at first, but it was so worth it. Many times the good stuff came after the crowds had left for the day. We all have to be careful.

> *I really like it when the Lord moves in signs and wonders. I like the healings. Everything He does is very special to me. I know that He uses me in that capacity as well. I get so zealous for it that I will quite often push to see it. The problem can be that it is possible that my zeal can come across as or be taken as a cockiness or an arrogance. I don't feel that way, and any time the Lord moves in a miraculous way I am very excited to see it. There can be other ministers of the gospel that don't press in for the miraculous as much as I do, so they don't see much of it. Additionally, they don't have a lot of patience for someone who does move in the miraculous, so they will tend to want to shut things down. It is unfortunate for the body. If they feel that they can be as effective without the Lord moving in miracles, signs, and wonders, then they can have at it. For me, I prefer to let the Lord do all of the heavy lifting, and then my job becomes hanging out like a groupie, admiring everything he does so much. When I see Him move and do things that would be impossible for me, I just love Him more.*

After everything pretty much wrapped up for the night we were headed out to the car. An older woman approached, and she said through the translator that she wanted prayer for her feet. The people here are like that, they won't move during the service when the anointing is flowing, they will wait until everything is over with, and then they want you to flow like you were still under the anointing. There is a difference, and the best thing to do is flow with the spirit of God, and move when He is moving. My initial reaction was again, no...we are done for the night. I have to get used to people wanting prayer after I think that I am done for the night. I must be the servant, and not react to it negatively in my mind. I wanted to go inside the church so that the anointing would be stronger, additionally, the ground outside was very dusty, and I didn't want to get dirt on my pants if I was led to kneel and lay hands on he feet.

The translator and I went back into the church to pray for this lady. She kind of hobbled when she walked, and I could see she was in some pain. After a few minutes of rebuking the pain, she said she felt much better. I told he to do something she couldn't do before. I took her by the hand and started to walk her back and forth in front of the stage. Then we started to trot and jog. I felt like a big time healing evangelist. I have seen this before several times. Honestly, I thought they faked it. It was just like you would see on TV, except we were pretty much the only ones in the church. I wasn't doing it for the cameras anyway, so it didn't matter. It just was interesting, and it caused me to think of televangelists I have seen in the past. The important thing is that the woman was healed, Praise God.

Thursday 8/28/08 Edo went to spend some time with her sister, I remained at the house and spent the day talking to Marcel, and checking email. The day was productive enough. I would have like to have had a vehicle so that I could go to the bank, try to find out a little about the diamond import and export business, and basically look around. It is rather difficult to travel because the driving is difficult, and I didn't want to wander into trouble. Marcel would be safe to travel with, but in a sense it would be a lot of responsibility for him, and I didn't want to put it all on his shoulders.

Sunday 8/31/08 Edo was speaking at the "Mount of Transfiguration" Church. After she spoke a few minutes, I had to leave with Pastor Jude so that I could speak at Mount Zion Church located in the Momma Mobutu neighborhood. I spoke on Genesis chapter two, and Adams relationship with the Father, and Jesus' job in restoring that relationship for us. I prayed for a lady that had a bad ear, and she said it was healed. Earlier I spoke about pressing in for your healing, then after the woman's ear was healed a man walked up to be prayed for about his stomach and his rotator cuff. He was pressing in like I spoke about earlier. The Lord healed his stomach, and his rotator cup. We ended up running out of time. I was ushered into the back where they provided some juice and allowed me rest a minute.

Several people then met me in the back for prayer. It was a Pastor and his wife, they wanted prayer so they could have children. He brought me a cash gift which was nice, and which was promptly spent on travel expenses. A woman came up complaining of paralysis in her ear area, no menstrual flow, as well as stomach trouble. I love it when they look so innocent, throw their hands up and ask for prayer. As soon as I laid hands on this woman, the demon manifested. Her whole body stiffened, her head went way back, her tongue curled up in her mouth, her hands clenched. She tried to twist away from me, but I wouldn't let up until the demon was out. Once it left, her head immediately felt better, and her stomach felt better too. That one was real satisfying. A real manifestation, and a relatively rapid and complete deliverance. She looked visibly relieved. Dr. Jude was amazed. It wasn't me, it was Jesus.

Pastor Jude and I returned to "Mount of Transfiguration" to pick up Edo then we all went home to rest.

Pastor Jude had found this little church with a dirt floor somewhere in Kinshasa. I have no idea where we were, or what the name of the church was. There were only about 50 people there. We were actually there for the first time on Saturday night, but Edo had an appointment and we left early. Saturday night was like the twilight zone. We went to this church, people were falling out all over the place. They were then carried out the back of the church because it was open. We would lay hands on people 99% of the time they would freak out under the power of God, and fall over backwards. The catchers wouldn't let them fall over on the spot, they were carried, or dragged, or pulled out the back of the church and then laid on the dirt. If we would continue to lay hands on them, they would continue to writhe about and cry and holler. It was the most pandemonium I had ever seen in any church anywhere. Then, to make the night more strange, without explanation, our entire group got up, got in the cars and we left. We then drove all over, momentarily met with Edo's cousin Tender, and then went home. I didn't know where I was and didn't know where we were going. It was a little different. I never did get the scoop on what all that was about.

This evening, we returned to the church that we abruptly left the night previous. Once again, it quickly got real wild. We had several altar calls, many people got prayed for two and three times for different things. People were falling under the power and were being dragged outside...the whole bit.

At the beginning of the service I saw in a vision three flower bouquets thrown on the ground. Then I saw a fire that was just coals and going out, that was surrounded by rocks. Then I saw something being sifted. I felt in my spirit that it was death and judgment I then felt that it was witchcraft against the church. I told the vision to Edo and she said she saw a car wreck and death also. We released it at the beginning of the service, and called for the repentance of the individuals involved... it was really good. We called out the witches, and told them that unless they repented, that their lives would be required of them. It was during the beginning of the service that I smelled hair burning. No one moved.

After the service, we prayed for everyone that wanted to repent, and then for everyone that wanted to be married, then babies, then childless couples, then laying on of hands for healing, then the terminally ill. The terminally ill turned into everyone that the doctors couldn't cure by translation error...so the 30 to 50 people I laid hands on for healing came back to be prayed for again. It was easier to just go along with it, so we did.

One of the people that I remember most was the woman with tuberculosis and heart trouble. She looked much better after prayer. She looked taller, and could take deep breaths. She also seemed very pleased. There were 5 or 6 women who said that they felt something in their wombs. Several people had me pray for them, and then had Edo pray for them; double dippers. One woman was the woman that was bitten by a dog, and said that she felt a snake in her belly. One woman had two operations for a tumor in her belly, and now it was back again. I cursed the tumor and rebuked it, she then reported that she felt heat in her belly. There was a little girl there that was about two years old, she had what looked like cataracts in her eyes. I prayed for them, and they seemed to clear up a little. I pressed in 3 times, but they eyes wouldn't go clear. I didn't feel the sensation of the Holy Ghost while in prayer for her, like I have before. If I felt the tingling, or the swelling in my hands it seems to be stronger. It is a learning experience understanding how the Holy Spirit talks to us.

Monday 9/01/08 We left late for Zion Church in the Mama Mobutu neighborhood, to make it more interesting the traffic was especially heavy. Evidentally they were waiting for us because when we arrived they immediately introduced Edo, and she started speaking. It is difficult to shift from traffic jams to things above, I have done it, and it is rough. She handled it fine though. The subject of her talk was "God is Unpredictable", and it was nice. After the lesson we shifted to the word of knowledge that I had about double vision. I guess you could call it the double vision vision. (Couldn't resist). All I saw was something that looked like the front windshield of a car with a rear view mirror, except that there were four rear view mirrors. It was like the rear window was split and everything was double. The vision was real quick, and it didn't repeat, and it wasn't real clear.

When I released the word, I only expected one person to respond because it seemed like an oddball word to release. Additionally, I expected that it was due to a car accident because of the rear view mirror, and the windshield that I saw. I also felt that it was a man. Two women and four men responded to the word of knowledge. I interviewed them quickly, looking for the one that was in the car accident. No one had a car accident, but one guy had an accident at work that caused his condition, so I started with him. After praying for and laying hands on all six, all six were healed. Of course no doctor could verify all of this at this time, so I had to take their word for it. In my mind, the people feel a certain pressure to say that they are healed, when in fact they are not because they might not want to appear they have doubt. I checked them pretty carefully as I went. The last guy said he was better, but he hesitated. I told him it was ok, and I prayed for him again. This time it seemed more cleared up, additionally he had an eye that was difficult for him to hold open and I could tell it was noticeably better. Praise God, 6 sets of eyes healed. At the end of the night quite a few people came up for various prayers. One guy had an eye he could barely see out of. He indicated he had perhaps 5% vision in that eye. I prayed for him, several times. Each time I prayed, he indicated it was a little better. I really pressed in on this one. He finally ended up with a 60% improvement. May the Lord Jesus have him continue to heal overnight, and as he testifies. Amen The Lord had victory at Zion.

After the six eyes were healed, we were out of time. We did a mass prayer for the people, especially any cancers or tumors. We had the people stand and place their hand on the part of their body where they needed a healing. After the prayer, I had Edo ask how many people felt heat or electricity in their bodies. More than 20 people raised their hands. I would have preferred to lay hands on all the people, but there just wasn't time. If the people were really pressing in, they managed to see us afterwards anyway. One young girl had sickle cell anemia and was facing a bone marrow transplant. Yikes, I wouldn't even want to go into a hospital here for a hangnail, let alone let them treat me for something serious.

One thing they did that was clever, they had us lay hands on people and bless them as they brought their offering. One thing was sure, they all at least walked by the offering basket. I think the offering was pretty strong today.

Tuesday 9/02/08 Today was the day that I went to the little church and led an evangelism outreach located in an area called Matete. I was ready to go at 9:30 am when the translator showed up. His name was Levy, Marcel's buddy the English tutor. That day he had an English lesson scheduled with one of his students. Since he needed to tell his student that the class was canceled, and because he didn't do it yet and as there was no other way to get in touch with the student, he ended up walking to the students house to tell him. He was back by 10 am. I was supposed to be at the church at 10:30.

One of Edo's Nieces was named Marissa. She was about three years old. She was a little nervous about me the first time she met me because I think I was the first white person she had ever seen. She was already nervous about me, and the family picked up on it, so they decided it would be funny if they picked her up and set her on my lap. Well, she started screaming and screaming, refusing to be comforted. They thought it was funny, but she never got over it. From then on, every time she saw me, she would start to cry. About the time Marcel's friend showed up, Marissa's mother showed up too. It turns out that Marissa's mother was headed downtown also. We ended up waiting around until they were ready to leave in order to save cab fare. Originally, Edo was going to have me take the Nissan, but after we thought about it, we decided it would be better to take a taxi so that we could avoid any potential trouble with the law. If they decided that I needed to be harassed for money, there wouldn't have been anyone there to handle them like she could. Law enforcement would occasionally ask me for some money for a soda, and I would usually give then 500 francs (less than a dollar) it was better for me to just keep them happy in case I needed anything.

We were running late, but by 11am we were already downtown. We drove right past the Kenya Airlines building and I wanted to double check the ticket. I was just paranoid about how they do things. So, we ended up stopping about two blocks before we should have so I could check the ticket. It only took a few minutes, and everything was fine, so it was a waste of time, except I felt better.

We finally got a cab. It seems that when a white man is around, the cab fare is much higher. It is like that all over the world, if you are from out of town, no problem, the fare goes up real quick and easy. We finally got a price we could live with, around $10.00 or double the going rate, take your pick. We finally got to the church by 12:30 pm. The driver couldn't find the church, and we had to stop and ask a couple of times. I couldn't remember even though I had been there before. We actually drove past the church, and I didn't even see it. At least the cab driver didn't charge any extra for all of the looking around that he did. I guess he felt that he had already gotten us pretty good.

When we arrived at the church for what was supposed to be a few hours of evangelism with the Pastor and one or two others had turned into an event. We were almost an hour late, and yet there were 40 to 50 people at the church. They were in full blown worship mode, so the atmosphere was set. I taught for a few minutes, I think I spoke about being sons of God, and divine healing. To the surprise of everyone (I could see it in their eyes) I told the church that we were all going out into the neighborhood and invite everyone to please come to the church and get prayed for. I went with the translator and the Pastor of the church. Apparently they had never done any real evangelism before. They seemed a little unsure of themselves.

The pastor had us stop at a few houses that were right next to the church. One of the houses was where a retarded boy lived. It was like a deaf and dumb spirit. I prayed fervently and tried to get it out, but it wouldn't leave. The boy wriggled around a bit as I prayed, he also resisted and tried to get away. After prayer, there was no real improvement. I asked the father to speak to the boy to see if he could talk. The father said " It is no use trying, the boy cannot speak." I see the problem...no faith. It is amazing how we think. Things are a certain way for a long time and we accept it as reality. Once you accept things the way they are instead of the way they should be, you are completely defeated. If this father had an ounce of faith, I think the boy would have been healed. I sure believed the Lord would heal him. Why not, He healed others.

We went to another house, and found a Catholic lady living there. She wouldn't come to the church because she was Catholic, she also said that she didn't need prayer. We then asked her if we could bless the house, and she let us. The point was really a meet and greet with the neighbors, along with an opportunity to tell them about Jesus. Really, we were just out looking for an opportunity to minister to others.

The next house was interesting. During the revival, the deaf heard, the blind saw, the poor had the gospel preached to them, and the dead were raised. The only thing we had missed was the cleansing of the lepers. I had realized that fact a day or two previous, and pointed it out to Edo, asking about any nearby leper colonies. I was also asking the Lord the day previous about lepers. I was doing this several times, just occasionally looking up and saying out loud, "OK Lord where are the lepers?" I did this at random times, and not usually privately. I was actually just trying to be funny about it. Perhaps it wasn't the best subject for humor, but then we are all growing, aren't we? There was a girl living in this house that had real hard rough skin patches on her hands and on her legs. It was like psoriasis, definitely a skin disease, and quite similar to leprosy. I began to pray, and the Spirit of the Lord hit her hard right away. Boom, she was out cold and had fallen over into the couch. It looked like it hurt, because the couch was broken, and didn't have any cushions on it. I believe she was healed, it just wasn't instantly.

We then proceeded back to the church. The crowd was beginning to gather. I prayed for about 75 to 100 people over about 3 hours. I felt it in my body for three days. It was exhausting work. One old man walked with a cane. He was also blind enough that he had to be led by the hand. He also had a stroke, so he had difficulty with one side of his body. I prayed for the paralysis. He slowly regained the use of his bad arm, but it didn't go to 100%. His blind eyes went to about 50% of normal. There was a second blind guy that said that he was in total darkness, and of course had to be led by the hand. I prayed for him several times, and each time he improved. At the end, he was about 50%. He could see well enough that he was able to go sit down by himself. When the man went by himself to sit down, everyone in the church got real excited. There were of course many other healings, like stomachs, female stuff, and on and on. Nothing else I could remember that was over the top.

Pastor Jude called several times throughout the day. About 1pm he called to say that he would be there in about two hours. He didn't show up until after dark. Pastor Jude was a wonderful man, and I knew he was really busy, and was doing everything he could to get there sooner, so it was good.

We quit about 4pm. I was pretty drained. The people kept coming, so finally we had to cut them off. Two women gave their lives to Christ. Afterwards, we went to the Pastors house, Pastor Timothy, and his wife. She prepared fish, thank you Jesus for healing me of the fish allergy. Pastor Tim had to go and prepare a lesson, so he left early. A short while later, Dr. Jude showed up. We then went to the Zion Church in the Mama Mobutu neighborhood for a meeting. The meeting went real well, and they really wanted me to come back another time. I finally got home by about 10:30 so we spent several hours involved in Pastor talk.

Wednesday 9/03/08 Edo was off on a cassava buying expedition. I went to the internet store, and then cleaned myself up and got ready for the day. Edo showed up to get me and was ready to leave again. I had the computer and was trying to burn a CD before we left. She wanted to take her laptop, so needed to wait until the next time it was available, and the power was on. First Edo went to meet with her husband Placide, then we went to see her Dad. We prayed for him, especially his eyes. They didn't get 100% better, but he did say that everything got real bright. He was a mess, diabetic, back problems, his hearing, his eyes. The Lord touched him, and he got upgraded, but he needed more help.

We Left Edo's dads house and went to The Zion Church to test our audio equipment. All of the equipment was in perfect working order. We finally left Zion about dark. A man that was there the last time we were there was in the church. He was the man that pressed in for his stomach, and his shoulder. He told us about a dream that he had. In the dream there was a white hand that came down, it was bloody and it touched his stomach. Honestly, when he said it was a white hand, I thought that he was referring to me, but then when he said it was bloody, I realized it was the Lord. Thank you Jesus for healing this man.

I was very tired by the time we got home. I had to lay down a few minutes before I had the energy to pray for everyone in the family before we left for civilization. By the time I got my things packed,and in bed it was already midnight.

Thursday 9/04/08 I don't like to get to the airport late, especially for international flights. The bottom line is that I was up and ready at 5:30 and ended up waiting until 6:15 for Edo and Regine. The driver showed up and checked the oil in the Nissan, which was low. The oil was so low that he felt that he needed to walk to the store and purchase the oil. By this time I am getting nervous because I wanted to be at the airport already. We finally left at 6:45 or so. We arrived at the airport at 7:15. A little late, but still ok. I really didn't want to find out what would happen if I missed this flight.

The Kinshasa airport is a zoo. Actually, it is wilder than that. People want to carry your bags for money, The guard won't let Edo in to help me unless they are bribed, I am sure that they make up taxes and fees. It cost $50 to get me through the airport in additional costs. It was very stressful for both of us. I forgot to say goodbye and smile at Edo's sisters as I left because I was so stressed out. I was trying to pay attention to everything, and I was following one of the porters. Before I realized it I had walked through the security doors without saying goodbye. Nothing I can do at that point, the entire experience is in the rear view mirror.

When I got to the waiting area, it turns out that I was the second person there. Another man came and set close by. I noticed that he was wearing a clerical collar. His name was Godwin Eze Okpunor from Benin (the country). After we got a good conversation going about the Lord, another man sat down near both of us. His name was Apostle Silas Oprince. We soon discover that the Lord had placed an Apostle, a Prophet, and an Evangelist in very close proximity. The conversation before we got on the plane was very good. Once we started to board the plane we walked about a block to get on the plane. When we got on the plane, we discovered that our assigned seats were right next to each other. We were all seated on the same row in a loaded 747 with about 300 passengers. That wasn't by chance. God has interesting ways to show that he is in various things if we will just pay attention.

I am now invited to Nigeria. Praise God. We fellowshipped all the way to Kenya. I got off in Kenya to go to London, and they continued on to Nigeria. I am now in the Kenya Airport and it is 21:42 local time. My flight is at 23:50. The divine connection with the Nigerian guys was interesting. *(Update: I am going to Nigeria in April of 2009)*

The Apostle said that by March the Lord was going to increase my anointing, and when I came to Nigeria my financial worries would be over. I kind of figured that. The Lord is setting me up nicely. Thank You Jesus. The prophet said there would be an increased anointing in three months. An anointing like Reinhardt Bonnke. Praise you Jesus. Sounds about right, the only question is how fast. Well, I wrote it down, and time will tell.

9/29/08 I am Finally back in the states. I have been here for awhile. Thank you Jesus for an amazing trip. On the way back from London, a woman on the plane was suffering from a severe migrane headache. I found out about it because the cabin steward was walking up and down the aisle asking for a doctor. I asked him what happened, and he asked me if I was a doctor. I said I was sort of in the medical profession. I finally decided that I should go and pray for her. She got better real quick, and was able to return to her own seat from the bathroom for the remainder of the flight. The crew knew what the Lord did, but most of the passengers didn't. They were extra gracious to me on the way off of the plane. God is Good.

Emails

THE following is a collection of emails that I sent from Congo. I decided to leave them as I sent them because it gives the full flavor of the experience. Writing an email from the Congo and getting it sent was always a race. Several times I took my time and wrote lengthy emails only to have the electricity suddenly go out. This crashed the computer causing me to lose all the work. I learned to type super fast, and to keep the emails short. The computers in the computer cafes were always old and worn out. The keyboards sometimes had keys that didn't work. The keyboards were also usually set up for Europe, France or Belgium. Therefore the keys were moved around to different locations. Because I was typing as fast as I could so I didn't lose the work, I made a lot of typo's. Sorry if that bothers you.

Re: more and more Congo Congo

Monday, July 21, 2008 12:24 PM

Hello,

I just wanted to drop you a note to tell you that I made it to the Congo safely, and that everything here is very good, the people are nice and I am in a safe place

So now for some of the details, I took Edo Mukeza o the airport in London because her flight was before mine. We ended up at the airport a little late. When we went to check in the whole thing was confusing and the British Airlines employees were not helpful. They kept giving wrong instructions. We got through all of that, and she went to go through security. Her carry on bag was exactly one half inch too big. Long story short , she missed the flight and had to go back in the morning. Now she is here ok, but one of her bags didn't make it. That is the bag with all of the speaker cables in it. BA is looking for it.

One of my bags was lost for a day, but it showed up today; All of the amplifiers will be here Wednesday or Thursday, and then we go to Kikwit for the first revival. Looks like we are going by car, and the roads are rough, so be it.

Pray to the Lord for a safe road trip, and that the rest of the equipment arrives on time. We are also short of speakers (the kind you need for the public address), so we need some provision there too.

I am getting used to eating tripe, not my favorite but it goes and stays down. The caterpillar like insect bugs that live underground were better than the tripe, but I still didn't eat many.

Everything is Good,

I Love You,

Andrew

Re: Greetings!

Thursday, July 24, 2008 9:44 AM

Hi.

Yesterday we shopped around for the rest of the equipment we needed for the revival, and now we have everything but the cables and the speakers. I bought the jacks, but I will have to solder them together once I figure out the deal on the wire. Everything is different here and they don't understand well because of the language difference, plus it is all a little technical.We are getting through it.

Today we left for Kikwit at 5am for the airport, the flight was at 6m by 9 am we left, while zondering around the airportm I took a picture and almost got arrested . I had to pay a ten dollar fine . it was just a ploy for the money. The qirport was cool. there were several broke down dc3s there that had been sitting a long time. Our plane looked pretty new, but when I went to step aboard, the stairs broke twice, while waiting to take off I noticed gasoline running out of one of the engines like a faucet on low, When I pointed it out, they said it always does that. and when we take off it will quit, Sure enough, but I think it just moved to another spot where we couldnt see it. We arrived in Kikwit just fine, thank you Jesus, and the welcoming delegation was there. The radio reporter 10 or more pastors, 20 or so singers, ten little girls who danced, about 50 other people in a long line waiting to be greeted. We went to town in a convoy of 10 cars with loudspeakers and the whole bit, The journey was about 8 miles and the streets were lined with people on both sides of the street the whole way, They were shouting and waving like a heros welcome for Edo. They told her that they are welcoming her, but they are really welcoming Jesus. I have never seen anything like it,

We are staying in an old hotel that used to be a convent or something. It is a little worn, but it will do, for the next few days, I will have internet available at least

Andrew

RE: REPLY

Monday, July 28, 2008 2:40 PM

Hi I need this message sent to a few folks, I will send a list in the next email

Hello,

I finally got to the internet so that I could report what has happened the last few days.

The second day of the crusade I felt that we should call the sick and infirm up to the front of the stage so that they could be in more of the anointing, and then pray for them at the end of the service, and then call Edo up to speak; Unfortunately there was some miscommunication and the people thought that God was going to work miracles for them right then, and about the time I introduced Edo, she was a little confused as well. It appered that I told everyone that God is great , and able to work miracles, and then I handed everything to Edo , so that He could. It was a difficult and funny moment. Edo spoke and her message was wonderful, she handled the confusion like a trooper. After she spoke, we started praying for the sick, The notable miracles were a deaf mute boy could hear, a woman that was carried to the revival has healed, and walked home, I also held and prayed for a sick baby that I think was healed of aids or something like that, and we prayed for another real sick woman and her sick baby, it was real touching.

The following day was the last day, and there was the largest crowd of 3 to 4000 people. Around 1000 people came to receive Christ as their savior. They were shoulder to shoulder 90 feet across, an 75 feet deep. So in total around 1600 people received Christ in the first city. We also had a muslim boy who also practiced witchcraft accept Jesus as Lord, and I found out todat that a man came to the revival to kill Edo with a Gun, but the power of God hit him, he started shaking and couldn't do it.

Also the head intercessor reported that they had a vision that the church where they were going to originally have the crusade was actually into witchcraft, so they moved the crusade; When they found out at the whitch church that it had been moved they sent poison food to the head intercessor. She got a vision about the poison food, and she kicked the food container in the vision, so when they showed up, she kicked the food container, the witches got in a car wreck on the way home and that was in the vision too, the leader broke his foot and his back.

Today was a little slower, we are just enjoying the Lords victory.

Andrew

Re: new e-mail address

Wednesday, July 30, 2008 3:19 AM

Hello,

We are leaving for Gungo pronounced goongoo this am. It is a 300km jeep drive all but the last 15km is paved. I dont know why you didnt get my last email, and I dont have time to fix it today. pls keep me posted about denise.

I love you,

Andrew

Ressurection life

Wednesday, August 6, 2008 3:37 PM

Hello All,

You are probably going to read this twice, and you are free to send it to anyone you want to.

In case you didnt get my previous email, I an currently working in an evangelism crusade in Democratic Republic of Congo, Africa ; We finished two weeks ago in Kikwit where we saw over a thousand people give their lives to Christ, including a muslim boy who was also into witchcraft. We also saw several notable miracles including a deaf mute boy who got his hearing, the speech will come now that he can hear.

In the book of John chapter 13 verse 15 Jesus said: For I gave you an example that you also should do as I did to you. V17 If you know these things you are blessed if you do them.

So, the story goes like this, and those of you who know me know that im telling the truth. I got a vision of diamonds when I was praying for the trip, and I realized that the Lord saw the value of the people here. The vision is longer than I care to type at this time, but when I was in Kikwit, the landscape matched the vision exactly. After that vision, but before I left for the trip, I got another vision, and this time I was washing the feet of the people here, literally. I wasn't sure exactly what it meant, and I didn't do it in Kikwit, so I decided after some soul searching and prayer that I would do it in Gungu. I felt the Lord was telling me that people would be healed if I did it, and it wasn't goung to cost anything but my pride. If people were saved and healed, that is what mattered.

Well, I didn't do it Friday because it was too hectic because we just got there, so I released it Saturday am in the morning conference and put it on the people to find exactly 10 lame people. Then the rest of the day I spent butting heads with the sound guys because they preferred loud sound instead of clear. Anyway, by the time the conference started, I had to go back to the hotel and clean up. I got back and I was tired and a little annoyed. Towards the end, Edo called for me and then announced that we needed 10 lame people. I really wanted wait for the next day, but the wheels were in motion. 10 lame came forward, and we set them on benches. I had the translator read john 13 about how Jesus washed the disciples feet, and then grabbed a big cloth, and wrapped it around myself. I asked the people if they wanted to see the love of God, and they went nuts, and then I asked if they wanted to see the power of God, and they went nuts again. I proceeded to wash their feet, asking them if they knew Jesus, and if they knew he loved them, and if He was their savior. Praying for their condition, and rebuking the devil off of their lives, and the lives of their families. Asking the Lord to heal them. And commanding their bodies to be healed. All told, there were two to three significant healings for people who could not walk, several dramatic improvements, and all but two walked away. Not bad, and well worth doing. There was also a girl who accepted Jesus as her savior. Interesting stuff, but it gets better.

The next day, Sunday morning, we got the news that Saturday while I was praying for one of the lame girls, her sister died. Apparently the girl left home, and was staying elsewhere and there was a bone with some string wrapped around it in her lotion, sounds like witchcraft, doesn't it.. She got real sick with typhoid and TB, but she got better, but then two weeks ago her two month old baby died. She then got real sick, couldn't eat, and finally died. Dead 30 minutes, and her bowels even released dead. By the way, she was under a nurses care, and the nurse verified it. The family was called, and the mourning had begun. Her mother was a praying woman, and she was praying at home for the girl, and the girl came back and died three times. The girl said quit praying, and the woman demanded to know who she was speaking with in the name of Jesus, because she didn't recognize the voice and the voice said Lucifer. So she commanded the devil to leave in the name of Jesus, the girl eventually recovered and we met with her Monday and did some prayer and deliverance on her. She said it felt like something lifted, and she felt better. By the way, I have her name and a videotaped testimony of her father, an eye witness. (on youtube)

So all told, the lame walked, the deaf heard, the dead were raised, and thousands gave their lives to Christ, not bad. Thank You Jesus.

Andrew

Re: Communication

Monday, August 11, 2008 6:38 AM

Hello All,

Well, I finally got a chance to sit down for a few minutes on a real computer and write of the events in and returning from Gungu. Thank You Jesus for the events that took place in Gungu, and the safe return. I knew that things would be good, that people would turn to the Lord, that healings would take place, that the kingdom of darkness would lose territory and be rebuked, I knew the Lord was good and His hand would move, but I have to confess that I did not see all that He had in store for us. I surely didn't think that the dead would be raised, and I didn't imagine having a part in it.

Just as a recap, around 3,000 people came out to hear Edo preach the gospel, and to tell her life story. Of the people in attendance, it was surprising to see how many children were there, it was perhaps as many as 500 children less than 12 years old. Of those in attendance perhaps 1,200 or so indicated that they wanted more of Jesus. The name of Edo's ministry is "Equipping the Hero's", so now that so many are hungry for the gospel we need to be knocking on heavens door requesting supplies like Bibles in the native tongues of Kicongo and Lingala, as well as French and English. Africa is such a vast project with so many opportunities to make a difference in peoples lives that the required materials to help in the spiritual as well as the material seems almost endless. Really, the thing to do would be to set up a teaching center that ran for 12 hours a day 7 days a week until the people got well grounded enough that it could be taken over by the local Body. Part of the problem is that well meaning western churches have come and given financial and material support in the past, and may even be doing it now, but the spirit of religion came with it, and it has established itself well in the churches. The local churches did some things that were surprising to me, like forbidding women from wearing pants, they did the collection in a manner of favouritism, so that those who gave the most went first, they even got real legalistic on a few doctrinal issues, fighting amongst themselves. Well, that is the past, and it could be ironed out with some in depth instruction, but the good that came out of this is that the local churches are all working together for the first time in a long time.

We waited in Gungu for two days before leaving so that we could rest up. Those two days were filled with people that had all kinds of requests. Mostly it centered on money, but a few had sicknesses and were looking for healing. Most of the sick either wanted you to take pity on them and give them some money, or to give them money for doctors or whatever medicines they wanted. I think some of them were truly disappointed when we prayed for them, but a few believed and received their healings, one lady got her back healed, there were some others also, Like the boy that suffered from epileptic seizures, I felt he was healed, The formerly dead girl who was resurrected got set free from demonic oppression and said she felt much better. The Lord was moving. Several people came and wanted us to fund projects like a farm, a home for widows, a home for orphans, a garage where people could be taught to be mechanics, you know, reasonable projects when one looks at it in the natural. Wisdom is wonderful, because the Lord was revealing the hidden motives of the heart as we went, and they didn't even realize it. He will also reveal when and how the funds will arrive and be dispursed at the correct time. It saves a lot of headache. It was a real productive couple of days because some people really needed some personal attention, and we were able to give it. It is amazing how many new friends you can make in a few days if they think that you are there to spend money. It is about the gospel first, then the rest should become self supporting.

God knows there is enough land with nothing on it waiting to be turned into farms, and made productive to feed the poor. The land is very inexpensive, and everything grows here. The problem is that people are thinking in the box. Citrus, avocados, mangos, bananas, coffee, coconuts, cattle, goats, chickens all grow here with very little effort. Of course one has to acquire the land and drill a well. After that it is just management. All in due time.

We left for Kikwit and Kinshasa Tuesday. 18 people in three vehicles. The land rover had three people crammed into the front seat. Our vehicle was the size of a Nissan pathfinder, and it carried 8, and the other vehicle was similar, and it carries 7. The ferry opened at 8am, and we were only a few minutes from the river. Once to the ferry it took about 1.5 hours to get all three vehicles across. We then proceeded to Kikwit on the jeep trail, it was bumpy and slow but by early afternoon we were in Kikwit. After buying more fuel, we proceeded to Kenshasa. The road started out paved, and there were hundreds and hundreds of people walking down the road in the middle of nowhere, on there way to and from Kikwit. We passed through many small villages and ran over a chicken two separate times. They don't seem to get it. Thank God we didn't hit any goats, we were not without opportunity to do so. By 10pm we hit a small town and stopped. I was informed that we were at the end of the good road. As soon as I got out of the car, all sorts of people came up to sell stuff, which seems to be the norm. I am looking for some sunglasses, and that hasn't happened yet for some reason. There is no shortage of dried eels and dried bugs on a stick. I prefer the bugs, they are smoked and quite good. Anyway, one of the first people I met was a gay guy. He wasn't selling anything outright, but I had a strong sense of the motives. He was wasting his time, he just hadn't figured it out yet. I am totally a target for all of the street vendors because they know I can afford it, they just don't understand how tired I am of the constant approach, and the persistence.

Around midnight we paid some kid to take us to the trail that lead to Kenshasa, and he rode on the spare tire of the suv in front of us. Real dangerous, but he didn't seem to care. I've seen people riding on the hood of cars going 50mph so what is the difference? As soon as we got to the trail head, we got stuck twice. They have these giant off road trucks that are like the all wheel drive 6 wheel army trucks. They make huge deep ruts in the sand, and the beginning was very sandy. They go so slow that if you run next to them, you can keep up easily. We spent two hours driving and getting stuck barely keeping in front of one of the large trucks. The production 4x4 vehicles cannot handle this terrain, more ground clearance is needed, and bigger tires. We lost our muffler around 2 am. After a difficult removal we proceeded till almost daybreak. At that time the other vehicle caught up to the land rover, that had gotten way ahead of us in the sand. That thing was slow on the road, but right at home in the bush. They stopped because they were losing their clutch. Well, thankfully they were able to proceed, and shortly thereafter the terrain changed into sand mixed with clay, so the base was harder. It was good for us too, because we also started having problems with our clutch slipping. We made it to pavement and then it was two hours into Kenshasa. At least we could pull a vehicle if we really needed to. I don't think it would have been possible in the sand. We finally made it home in Kenshasa by close to noon. About a 30 hour jeep ride. We were all exhausted and glad to be back. There were plenty of broken down vehicles along the way because it cost more to retrieve them that it did to abandon them. It was over 100 miles of nothing but goat villages and sand. Calling a tow truck or a mechanic is impossible. The smaller vehicles could probably be towed out by the big trucks, but I don't know how that would work either. Thanks to God we got out in one piece with no serious mechanical troubles. Parts are very hard to come by.

We have rested the past few days, and I think another series of conferences is coming up later this week. Stay tuned for the update.

RE: HI

WEDNESDAY, AUGUST 13, 2008 11:34 AM

Hi,

Everything is ok. We are getting set for some meetings in the next few weeks. So we are basically resting and doing some light running around. I will let you know about it all in a few days.

Thank for everything,

Love you lots ,

Andrew

RE: HI...AGAIN

FRIDAY, AUGUST 15, 2008 7:20 AM

Hi,

Please add the following emails to your list.

_____@hotmail.com
_____@yahoo.com

Hello Everybody,

Well. I had an interesting day yesterday. It started out with a detailed vision of the service tonight. Im not going to type all of the details, but it looks like ear night. The Lord showed me a woman at the service, where she was sitting, that she was deaf in at least one ear, possibly both, that she had someone to help her, how to pray for her, what she was wearing, how old she was, the whole bit. Looks like someones hearing is going to be restored. Then a wave of ear healings will follow.

We then went to an influential and sucessful pastors house. He must be doing well because a mercedes, an audi and a big house. The Lord gave me a vision of a black woman receiving a gift of a gold necklace with a pearl pendant. She was happy, and then she danced with a man and they were both happy. I asked the pastor if he had an anniversary coming, and he did, so I told him the vision. He was excited because he was wondering what to get his wife. I know that the Lord was creating favor for Edo and I, and even if he doesnt like us [which he does] his wife surely will. Plus the congregation cant squawk because the pastor can honestly tell the people it was from the Lord.

While I was in the US I really felt a strong strong need for sunblock, so I bought a bottle. I even was momentarily thinking to get it here in africa and save the trouble of carrying it, then I woke up. They dont need it here. Well in Gungu there was a girl at the church that was an albino, so then I realised why I needed the sunblock so desparately, so I gave it to her. Well I have been excited all along about the hydroelectric potential of the congo because they have 13 pct of the worlds hydroelectric potential. I have been thinking about it and thinking about small systems the whole time in my head. Just interested and curious about it. For those of you who know me well, you know that is something I would find interesting anyway. Yesterday we went to pray with a man, he was on the 15th floor of the water department. Come to find out he is the department head in charge of hydroelectric energy for the country. I have also met the man that licenses all of the cell phones, radio and TV stations in the country. So, a radio broadcast license is no problem. Why do you suppose the Lord has me meeting these people? In case you dont know, he is wanting to fix some things here.

Anyway,

I am getting ready for ear night, so its time to get going.

God Bless.

Andrew

HELLO

Monday, August 18, 2008 7:05 AM

Hi,

Just a quick update. Everything is going pretty well. Edo spoke in four different Churches Sunday. It got to be tiring at the end, but it went well.

The update on the ear lady is this, we went to the church and Edo testified what God did in her life. Afterwards, I gave the word of knowedge that I had for the woman, I felt very confident that she would be healed, so I was really looking forward to it. Well, the woman was there, but she had to leave early at 7pm, so we were informed that she already left. We were coming back Sunday, so I suppose it was ok. Sunday evening we were there again and I felt led to teach a few minutes on healing, so I did. After that I repeated the word of knowledge and again this woman was not there. We spoke to her daughter, and since Edo had a work of knowledge with no response we found out that apparently it was for the same person.

We had to leave and go to another church, so when I realized she wasnt there, we left rather quickly. Edo spoke again at the other Church, and on the way home we stopped. I found out that we were at the womans home. A miracle house call. It was a very large house in a nice area, so the woman vas fairly well off comparitively. Well, I wasnt really sure what was going to happen because the vision was actually at the Church, but why not. It is the Lord that heals anyway, and He can do it however He wants. I had the woman stand up, like in the vision, and asked her if she believed that Jesus would heal her, she answered in the affirmative, so I asked her if she believed Jesus would heal her now. She said yes again, so I placed my hands over her ears, like in the vision, and prayed for her ears to be opened, and rebuked the devil off of her life, and rebuked the deaf and dumb spirit off of her, and whatever else I could think of. Edo prayed in the same vein as well. When I couldnt think of anything else to pray, I removed my hands and asked her which ear was deaf. I was suppose to ask that first, but I forgot. She indicated the left ear, we tested it, and it was now fine/ Praise God. I asked her if the volume was the same, and she said that it was a little different, so I prayed again for good measure. Thank God for what He does.

OK,
 That is about it.

God Bless,

 Andrew

UPDATE

Friday, August 22, 2008 9:04 AM

Hello;

So here are the latest updates.

We went to a church (the one down a big hill) on Sunday; Edo spoke and we prayed for a bunch of people there. One was a very sick woman who was essentially carried there a few days ago. We had prayed for her at that time. When we returned Sunday she had walked to church and reported that she was doing much better. Praise God.

There was another woman that carried a photo of a boy and reported that the boy had been in a coma for awhile Edo and I Laid hands on the photo and prayed for the boy. It was reported a few days later that he had come out of the coma. Thank You Jesus.

Wednesday night we went to a Church near where Edos sister lived. It was nice because they didnt have a time limit and we were able to pray for everyone there. Also as Edo spoke; the sound system played outdoors and as the evening progresses more and more people came to listen. At the end about 15 people gave their lives to the Lord. We did some deliverance and prayed for everyone but I dont remember any notable instant healings. Im sure the Lord was healing and it is hard for me to get what is going on because of the language problem. One woman wanted prayer because her knees were hurting. I prayed for her and afterwards I asked her if she felt anything. Before the translator could ask her the Spirit of the Lord hit her and she began jumping all around. I never did find out about her knees. It is kind of like that here they get healed and then walk off without telling the translator what happened. I am going to get someone to interview and get names next time. Isnt it interesting that the Spirit of the Lord hits them even though I am praying in english and they dont understand me.

Last night we went to another Church and I felt that the Lord waned to do some miracles in the ears and tumors because he reminded me of those healings before we started. After Edo spoke she asked me if I wanted to say anything; so I told her about the miracles, so I reeased to the people that the Lord reminded me of healings in ears and tumors; and that He wanted to move in that area. They are always slow to respond, like they are shy. Once a few move, the rest come. In total about 50 people.

I prayed for a small boy, about 9 yrs old. Totally deaf in one ear. I asked him if he knew Jesus, and if he believed Jesus could heal him right now. He said yes, so I prayed for him. His ear was instantly healed. Praise God. Ears are nice because the result is right now and obvious. Another small boy about 2 was there with his mother, deaf in one ear. No point in interviewing this one, and his mother already indicated faith y coming forward. Well, he is not deaf now, I placed a finger in his good ear, his moher asked him a question in the other ear, and he answered. Thank You Jesus

I also prayed for an older woman about her hearing; it was healed as well; Thank you Jesus.

There was another woman that had cataracts and couldnt see well. She indicated after prayer that her eyes were fine now. Cataracts must bow the knee to Jesus, because He is Lord of all.

There were some oher things the Lord did, but do to the language problem I didnt get the details. There are also things the Lord does tha we dont get the report for a few days, like the coma story.

So, things are going well. The Lord is moving in signs and wonders. Speaking of wonders, Edo woke up Thursday am covered in gold dust on one hand, it was real early so she got up and knocked on my door and showed it to me and then we both went back to sleep since it was so early. By the time we got moving around; it was gone.

Anyway,

Thanks everyone for your prayers and support;

God Bless,

Andrew

Hello

Monday, August 25, 2008 9:08 AM

Hi Mom;

sorry to hear about Auntie Ruth. I guess it was really a matter of time. She had a really long life; and pretty healthy too. Anyway. I hope it is not too much addl stress on you.

You can send out the following. Try to add Dads address also; He will like this story

We went friday and saturday to a church near the small airport in Kinshasa. It is the church where Edos cousin Regine goes. The bottom line is that I heard the poop about the infidelity of one of the leaders wives; and some of the congregation too. I knew the Lord was going to use us to clean it up, but I wasnt sure how. The first night was rough; Edo gave her testimony and gave an invitation and not a soul moved. Very unusual. Another pastor spoke for a few minutes and finally they came up for prayer. There was a heaviness and an oppression on the people; from having a heavy burden for a long time. We prayed and some of it broke off; but we both knew there was more work to do on Sunday.

One of the interesting things that happened saturday was that a woman was in the prayer line and when she came up to be prayed for she touched her eyes and said something. I asked the interpreter and he said that she had a black spot on her vision. I felt that she had either a detached retina, or macular degeneration. Anyway I prayed for her and her vision improved. She went to leave; and I asked her if it was 100 pct and she said no: so I prayed again and it went to 100 pct healed. I have the video. Praise God. He is still in the healing busiess. So then another woman came up to be prayed for her blind eye ; It was weeping and had been like that for years. She had some kind of a spot on the white of her eye. She didnt get much improvement. I told her to come back the next day; and we prayed again; and she said she felt a little better; but I couldnt get it to leave: God heals how and when He wants to; I understand it but I still would like to see it be 100 pct.

The Spirit of the Lord moved on a bunch of people; there was deliverance and emotional healing all over the place. People being touched, falling under the power, Getting set free. There was a lot of stuff broken off of that Church and they will never be the same. The devil lost a lot territory Sunday.

Thanks for your prayes and support;

God Bless

Andrew

The eyes have it

Wednesday, September 3, 2008 4:24 AM

Hello,

The last few days have been interesting. I went with Edo to a church called the Zion Church. It was nice and there were about 150 people there. Before I arrived, the Lord showed me a quick vision where everything in the vision was double. It was a double vision vision.:) Anyway, I felt that I was supposed to pray for someone that had double vision. I told everyone in the congregation with double vision to come forward for prayer. I expected one or two, 4 men and 2 women came forward. I interviewed them before the prayer to make sure they all had double vision, they all said they saw two of everything. I prayed for them one at a time and afterwards asked them about there vision. They were all healed completely. Praise God

After the service a man came forward to tell me he was blind in his right. eye. He reported that he had 5pct vision in that eye. I prayed for him several times, and each time there was improvement. He finally estimated his vision was 60pct of his good eye. Praise God.

Yesterday I was at a little church doing an evangelization outreach, praying for people in the area that wanted prayer. We went around searching for people to pray for, and brought them to the church. The first guy was totally blind in the dark and was lead in by the hand. I had to pray for him several times as well, although he could see shadows at the end and wasnt able to be 100pct, he was able to find his seat by himself. Thank You Jesus

The next blind guy was there for his paralysis, the Lord had me pray for the paralysis,(it looked like a stroke) and he got a big improvement, but not a total healing. I noticed his eyes and he reported that his vision was very poor he could barely see and was lead by the hand also. I prayed for him and his vision got good enough he could walk around by himself. In fairness, the third guy was totally blind, and although I prayed for him several times, he did not improve. The Lord can heal who He wants, and the healings are His business, so I dont worry about what doesnt happen and I am thankful for what does.

Things are going good, and I return to london tomorrow,

UPDATE

Friday, September 5, 2008 7:37 AM

Hello,

I am back in the UK, so it is possible to get internet access that is high speed, and computers that stay working. YEAH!!!! Im busy uploading my videos to to youtube. They are some classics, bug eating, the resurrected girl, shots of the revival. Good stuff.

Here is the link.

http://www.youtube.com/profile_videos?user=africarevival

The flight wasn't too bad, the plane was a 777. The only problem was the 6 hour layover in Nairobi. The good news is that I am bringing back $50,000,000 fifty million dollars with me. The bad news is that it is money from Zimbabwe, and it is worth less than a dollar.

I will send out a recap of the whole trip as soon as I can.

Andrew

UPDATE..PLEASE SEND IT OUT TO THE LIST.

Saturday, September 13, 2008 10:32 AM

Hello,

The following is a short summary of the highlights of the revival that I worked at in the Congo . (Zaire) It was a big adventure, and although I am glad to be back in the states, I feel that the work has just begun.

The adventure really started at the Lakeland Outpouring, a revival and healing outpouring in Lakeland Florida that started on April 2nd, 2008. During the outpouring I saw that many other revivals would trace their roots to this revival. At the revival in Lakeland I met a woman named Edo Mukeza who was from the Democratic Republic of the Congo , We got to know each other a little bit during the week she was there. She told me that she was going to the Congo by herself and putting on a revival. Well, that is a lot for one person, and the Lord put it on my heart to help. To make a long story short, I found my self in the Congo . The expected attendance was estimated to be between 6,000 to 30,000 people per night. The revival consisted of 3 days in Kikwit, a city of about 300,000, and 3 days in Gungu, a city of about 100,000. There were to be many other opportunities to minister scattered around during the six weeks that I planned to be in the Congo .

As you can imagine there were quite a few difficulties that were encountered during this trip. The problem was primarily the lack of infrastructure in the country. There were also some difficulties with language and culture. The Lord guided us through all of the difficulties, and the revival pretty much went as planned. The first city was Kikwit, Edo and I spoke to and ministered to a crowd of about 6,000 people. Around 1,200 people in Kikwit either accepted Jesus as Lord, or rededicated their lives as a result of this campaign. We were working with all of the local churches, so they were there to do the follow up, which was wonderful. We saw several notable healings as well. One boy about 12 or so was totally deaf, and could not speak as a result. He can now hear. Another woman was paralyzed and was carried to the revival, she walked home.

Gungu was the next city we visited. Again we had about 1,200 people come to the Lord for salvation. Before I arrived in Gungu, the Lord showed me a vision where I was washing the feet of the lame. I did it the second night, and we had some wonderful healings. One is on you tube, do a search for "Africa Revival" and you will see several videos. One of the videos on you tube is of the dead girl, after she was resurrected. She died while I was washing the feet, and the family sent people to the revival to tell her sister. Her sister was one of the lame people I was praying for, so they fortunately couldn't get to her. I prayed for her feet, and also rebuked satan off of her life as well as the lives of her family. Due to the grace that was on the city as a result of the revival, and due to the prayers that Edo and I made and due to the fact that the girl had a praying mother that was asking the Lord for a resurrection, the girl is still with us, after being dead 30 minutes. She was at a clinic when she died, and the medical people there verified it. Praise God.

When we returned to Kinshasa , we worked in different Churches almost every night. The Lord continued to pour out his grace, and we saw many other healings, miracles and deliverances. The deaf heard, the blind saw, demons were cast out, and the poor had the gospel preached to them. I realized that no lepers were cleansed, so I mentioned it to Edo, and to the Lord, and the next day I had the opportunity to pray for a woman that had a skin disease that caused her skin to be very rough. She fell over under the power of God almost as soon as I began to pray for her. She was probably healed, but it wasn't instantly.

Edo's ministry is called equipping the hero's, and now that many people have been won to the Lord, I feel an obligation to further equip them with Bibles, teaching materials, and support. I am also already in the planning stages for next year. I am making time available to share with other believers about this experience. Please contact me if you have an interest.

Andrew Snyder

Conclusion

LET us hear the conclusion of the whole matter: Fear God, and keep his commandments: for this is the whole duty of man. Ecclesiastes 12:13 (KJV)

In Conclusion, you should now be able to see how God moves in our lives. He is at work on all of us, some of us are stubborn and slow to listen, but He is still at work on and in us. I didn't ever believe at the beginning of my life that I would be where I am now. I am sure that Edo shares my experience. God has His ways directing our steps by putting obstacles in our path or giving us situations that we have to go through in our lives. This is so that we can be drawn closer to Him. Trials can be for our correction.

The Bible says:

11My son, despise not the chastening of the LORD; neither be weary of his correction: 12For whom the LORD loveth he correcteth; even as a father the son in whom he delighteth.

Proverbs 3:11-12 KJV

9Furthermore we have had fathers of our flesh which corrected us, and we gave them reverence: shall we not much rather be in subjection unto the Father of spirits, and live? 10For they verily for a few days chastened us after their own pleasure; but he for our profit, that we might be partakers of his holiness. 11Now no chastening for the present seemeth to be joyous, but grievous: nevertheless afterward it yieldeth the peaceable fruit of righteousness unto them which are exercised thereby.

Hebrews 12:9-11 KJV

Edo Mukeza went through some stuff in order to become who she is today, Andrew Snyder went through some stuff as well. We all have trials and difficulties we have to go through because it is a part of the lessons that we have to learn so that we can grow into who we need to become. This is so that we can adequately handle the circumstances that we are called and destined to handle. The chastisement is designed to draw out the best in us.

The Bible also says:

"28And we know that all things work together for good to them that love God, to them who are the called according to his purpose."

Romand 8:28 KJV

"9Remember the former things of old: for I am God, and there is none else; I am God, and there is none like me, 10Declaring the end from the beginning, and from ancient times the things that are not yet done, saying, My counsel shall stand, and I will do all my pleasure:"

Isaiah 46:9-11 KJV

"4Then the word of the LORD came unto me, saying, 5Before I formed thee in the belly I knew thee; and before thou camest forth out of the womb I sanctified thee, and I ordained thee a prophet unto the nations."

Jeremiah 1:4-6 KJV

God knows the end from the beginning. He knows everything that we ever have or ever will go through. He is not surprised by anything going on in our lives. He has everything in our lives orchestrated to bring the best out of us. Trust Him, God has everything all worked out already. From the beginning of time He knew us. Before we were born, He knew us. These things He has worked out are for our growth, training and correction. Do not fear or be dismayed, God is in control.

I do not care what you are going through now. God is able to handle it if we will put our trust in Him. There are circumstances and problems that we have to go through. Sometimes they are for our own good, sometimes we go through them for the good of others. This is so that we can be God's instrument to meet other people at the point of their need for the purpose of encouraging them and ministering to their needs. It is difficult to see when you are going through it, but when you get through and look back it is so that God's purpose can be realized in your life and in the lives of the people around you.

God has things he wants to do with you. I know it can be hard to believe if you base it on where you are now, but it is the truth. God has miracles He wants to do through you, He has people He wants to touch, He has people He wants to save,He has revivals he wants to do, He has churches he wants to start, build and edify through you. He does everything through people.

> "4In all my prayers for all of you, I always pray with joy 5because of your partnership in the gospel from the first day until now, 6being confident of this, that he who began a good work in you will carry it on to completion until the day of Christ Jesus."
>
> Philippians 1:4-6 NIV

Paul, in the book of Philippians calls it a partnership in the Gospel. Jesus did his part on the cross, and we are to do our part on the earth. In the New Testament, when God wanted to reach a man with the Gospel, He always sent a man to do it. For example, we read about the conversion of the Ethiopian Eunuch in the Acts of the Apostles chapter 8 starting at verse 26. We read in verse 35 that "Philip opened his mouth, and began at the same scripture, and preached unto him Jesus." It was possible for God to reach the Ethiopian Eunuch with the Gospel in many different ways, but he chose to use a man to do the job.

In The book of Acts chapter 9 we read about the conversion of Saul of Tarsus. Saul was busy plotting the murder of Christians and while he was on the road to Damascus, Jesus appeared to him. In verse 6 we read "6And he trembling and astonished said, Lord, what wilt thou have me to do? And the Lord said unto him, Arise, and go into the city, and it shall be told thee what thou must do." Acts 9:6 KJV Jesus didn't tell Saul what to do, he sent Annanias, and he told Saul what to do. God uses people, that is our part, allowing Him to use us to reach people.

> "17And Ananias went his way, and entered into the house; and putting his hands on him said, Brother Saul, the Lord, even Jesus, that appeared unto thee in the way as thou camest, hath sent me, that thou mightest receive thy sight, and be filled with the Holy Ghost. 18And immediately there fell from his eyes as it had been scales: and he received sight forthwith, and arose, and was baptized."
>
> Acts 9:17-18 KJV

God uses people to reach and touch other people. You have to go through different experiences, but the experiences are not without purpose. Everything is for a reason, there are no accidents with God. Do not lose heart if you are Going through something now, God designed it to make you a better person.

This book may be for a special purpose in your life. I know I was lead to write it. I do not know where all of the copies of the book are going, or who will see them or what they will accomplish in all of the lives of the people who see this work. God knows. He has orchestrated circumstances in both of our lives in such a way that our paths have crossed for a purpose. Do not let that purpose pass you by. If you are going through something, let this book minister to you. If you are supposed to preach the Gospel to the poor in person or by sponsoring some revivals, then be obedient to what God is telling you. If the purpose of this book is to lead you to salvation, then that is wonderful too.

Conclusion

Salvation is a personal experience. God is not doing production work. He doesn't present Himself to everyone the exact same way. He is doing custom work. We are all unique and individual, we are all called to different areas and ministries. God has selected you for His purpose. We still have our free will, and we can reject Him, but we are still called. He will present Himself to you in whatever way He has to in order to get your attention. Some people can just come to the still small voice, others it takes an earthquake to get their attention. God will get your attention one way or the other. That is why Jesus said " He who has an ear to hear, let him hear." It is better to hear the still small voice, than to wait for the earthquake.

The first step towards salvation is belief. Without belief, nothing moves. The Bible says in Romans 10:17 "So then faith cometh by hearing, and hearing by the word of God." KJV There has been enough testimony to the goodness of God and to the works of His hand in this book to bring you to a point that you have to know that God is, and that He is a rewarder of those who diligently seek Him. (see Hebrews 11:6) Even so, for some people, a mountain of evidence is not enough. The issue is not the quality or the quantity of evidence, the issue is that if they admit that they believe in God, then they would have to change their lives and admit they are wrong.

Once a person comes to a point in their lives that they are willing to admit that there is a God, and that man is not the highest being in the universe, then people have to change their ways. In Romans chapter 3:23 the Bible says "For all have sinned, and come short of the glory of God;"KJV The issue is that once we acknowledge God then we also have to admit our sins. Sin is an ugly thing. It encompasses all that we have done to hurt our fellow man as well as all that we have done to ignore God and the wonderful atoning work he has done on our behalf on Calvary. Since we have now become painfully aware of our sins, we also realize that something has to be done to make them go away so that we no longer carry the burden of guilt and shame. Thanks be to God for the work on calvary's tree. God has made arrangements to take away the burden guilt and shame of sin, through faith in Christ as out Savior.

Repentance. Repentance is the next step. It is essentially telling God that we are sorry for what we have done in the past and that we will make an effort to never do it again. It really deals with a heart issue, we want to quit and we feel sorry and remorseful for our sins, but we cannot seem to find the strength to give it up. Actually, we do not have the strength in us as human beings to quit sin. Paul said a mouthful in Romans 7:14-25

> 14For we know that the law is spiritual: but I am carnal, sold under sin. 15For that which I do I allow not: for what I would, that do I not; but what I hate, that do I. 16If then I do that which I would not, I consent unto the law that it is good. 17Now then it is no more I that do it, but sin that dwelleth in me. 18For I know that in me (that is, in my flesh,) dwelleth no good thing: for to will is present with me; but how to perform that which is good I find not. 19For the good that I would I do not: but the evil which I would not, that I do. 20Now if I do that I would not, it is no more I that do it, but sin that dwelleth in me. 21I find then a law, that, when I would do good, evil is present with me. 22For I delight in the law of God after the inward man: 23But I see another law in my members, warring against the law of my mind, and bringing me into captivity to the law of sin which is in my members. 24O wretched man that I am! who shall deliver me from the body of this death? 25I thank God through Jesus Christ our Lord. So then with the mind I myself serve the law of God; but with the flesh the law of sin. KJV

He is essentially saying that we can recognize good, and that God and the law of God is good, but we are powerless to follow the law completely and to do good exclusively. Repentance is a process, moving away from sin and the desires of this world and moving towards God. It is an about face, or a U-turn moving in the opposite direction from the way we once were going. Repentance as a process means that repentance is not a one time only event, then we are free to live however we want to until we feel like repenting again. John the Baptist said " Bring forth fruit in keeping with repentance" In other words don't repent for the show, or for the moment, continue to repent until your life becomes fruitful.

There is so much to teach concerning salvation. I could write another book on the subject. We have not covered the good confession, like when Peter confessed that Jesus is the Christ, the Annointed on, the Son of the Living God in Matthew 16:16. See also the conversion of the Phillippian Jailer in Acts, where the Jailer confessed Christ. We have not covered Baptisms in water for the remission of sins, or Baptism in the Holy Ghost. We have not covered the sinners prayer. We have not discussed walking faithfully with Jesus. We have not discussed Judgement. We have not discussed the atoning blood of Christ. There is just too many subjects that need to be covered, and there isn't time or space to cover them adequately here. Ask God to direct your steps to a Spirit filled church that is full of His people. He is faithful, and He will do it. "Seek and ye shall find" It is a beautiful promise in the Bible.

> 40And with many other words did he testify and exhort, saying, Save yourselves from this untoward (evil) generation.
>
> Acts 2:40KJV

I used to mock people when they spoke of "getting saved". Saved from what? I used to say. I will tell you what from, from a horrible existence on this earth without God, followed by a worse existence in eternity without God. Get Saved.

That is the point, "Fear God and keep His commandments" "Save Yourselves". Life is shorter than you think. People think that they can wait until the 11th hour in their lives to accept Jesus. I have seen a lot of elderly people. They die slowly in the nursing home. They are either slowly losing their minds due to Alzheimers, or they are doped up on pain killers. Either way, they are no longer in a mental state such that the government recognizes their ability to decide things for themselves. Do you think that after a lifetime of rejecting Jesus that they are going to suddenly be in a strong enough mental state to decide to follow Jesus? I would hope so, but the reality of the situation is that they basically aren't. That is why I am not a fan of death bed conversions. First of all, you may not get the chance, and second of all, you may not be mentally able to even if you do get the chance. The time to get it right is right now!

The young mostly die suddenly, car wrecks, accidents and the like. Do you think that you are going to be so fortunate as to have the time to make it right with God before you go. I would hope so, but the reason why you waited until the pressure is on is because you were not sincere in the first place. Do you think that God is a fool? He sees right through your insincere rush to get it right with Him. People come to God because they are dying, then when they get the all clear, they forget what they told God that they were going to do when they were dying. The worst type of deceit is self deceit. That is when we lie to ourselves, telling ourselves we have time. I will do it after I graduate, or when I get married, or when I retire and I have time for God. Who promised you these things? Today is the day of salvation. Humble yourself and come to God on His terms.

God Bless you. I pray that the words in this book will lead you to a deeper, fuller and more satisfying walk with the Lord and Savior Jesus Christ.

Amen

To see photos of the revival please visit www.africarevival.com.

To contact the ministry visit the website or email us at africarevival@gmail.com

www.ingramcontent.com/pod-product-compliance
Lightning Source LLC
Chambersburg PA
CBHW061651040426
42446CB00010B/1685